You Can't Do That!

By Ms. Cellaneous, The Unknown Attorney

Bellissima Publishing, LLC
Jamul, California
www.bellissimapublishing.com

Copyright © 2010 by Penny D. Weigand

All rights reserved. No part of this book may be reproduced or transmitted in any form or by any means, electronic or mechanical, including any photocopying, or recording, or by any information or storage retrieval system, without permission from the publisher and author.

LEGAL DISCLAIMER

This book is the opinion of one attorney only and is not intended to give specific advice on any area of the law. For specific advice on any legal matter, please consult your own attorney. Laws not only change, they also vary from state to state.

IBSN 978-1-935630-38-8
First Edition

To Art Margolis
and to My good friend and mentor,
the Late ROBERT (Bob) Deems

Introduction

The law is a good thing, and man has been compiling laws and rules in one way or another since time immemorial. This book is meant for California attorneys, but anyone anywhere can enjoy this book, because it is based on a system of right.

Everyone loves to hate lawyers and taxes, and people say the only thing you can be sure about is death and taxes; so what this means is people cannot be sure about attorneys. This book attempts to change all that, to change the state of the world, by bringing attention to a few things called morality and integrity.

Ms. Cellaneous, The Unknown Attorney, loves right and justice. This is her third book on the law. Her first book, "Everything You Never Wanted To Know About Your Nonprofit Corporation," was used as a textbook in a graduate class in public management at BYU, Utah. This book was written to complement a CLE course she's teaching for Lawline on line as one of their on line professors.

This book is informative and serious and fun, and will point out some real life experiences The Unknown Attorney has had in her own law practice. Who is The Unknown Attorney? Turn to the copyright page in this book to find out. This book is about doing what is right, and about following the rules and about defining integrity and justice.

Frederick Augustus Washington Bailey, who later became known as Frederick Douglass once said, "Where justice is denied, where poverty is enforced, where ignorance prevails, and where any one class is made to feel that society is an organized conspiracy to oppress, rob and degrade them, neither persons nor property will be safe."

Fredrick Douglass was born a slave; and with those words, he said it all.

You Can't Do That!

*By Ms. Cellaneous,
The Unknown Attorney*

You Can't Do That!

CHAPTER ONE

Why Can't We All Just get along?

The thing about the legal rules of ethics is that they are really supposed to teach us the common sense of doing what is right. I once had a law school professor tell me that when you become a lawyer and think like a lawyer your version of right and wrong changes because it becomes based in the law. Apparently, becoming a lawyer rewrites your past, or something.

I could not disagree more. I think you come into the legal profession with whom you are, and the law somehow gets pasted onto or into that. If you were a rude jerk *before* you became a lawyer, you will remain one *after* you become a lawyer. This is why the ABA Rules of Professional Conduct were created and why the various state bars have adopted their own versions of these rules. . .

to give all the jerks who are now attorneys some sort of ten commandments of behavior, and in this case there are just a lot more of those commandments.

The unfortunate thing is that instead of using these rules to monitor themselves, attorneys have turned and used them against one another in the form of threats used to manipulate a legal position and through other means.

I know this is true because during my somewhat long tenure as an attorney I think I have either seen every rule broken, or have had every dirty trick in the book used against me, including wrongfully reporting me to the state bar (more on that later).

The bottom line is you must trust no one. This is no longer a gentlemen's profession, and if the other guy thinks he can get away with something, he will. The term vigorous advocacy has become confused with "anything goes as long as I don't get caught," and good guys think twice about reporting things to the state bar because they realize you have to practice law from year to year and not day to day, or even month to month.

An outcropping of these new attitudes has been the resultant creation of the California Rules of Professionalism and Civility and the Civility Toolbox, a sort of "Miss Manners" handbook for the lunkheads.

These were adopted in 2007, not too soon for the attorneys of California, who are more often than not, anything but civil.

You Can't Do That!

The good attorney will not need to even read these rules, because he or she should be practicing them from day to day because he or she *plans* on working with opposing counsel from year to year.

However, the question becomes has the legal profession grown so large, and are there so many attorneys out there that you may see an opposing counsel only once in ten years (on one case) or never see the opposing counsel again. The mantra becomes "anything goes." And are there so many attorneys out there competing for the dollar that they will do anything the client says and thereby breach their duty to the court?

This book will take a look at various points in the California Rules of Professional Conduct and the new California "Civility Toolbox" in an attempt to both alert counsel of danger signs and to make sense of the quagmire into which we have all apparently fallen.

I tell people going into the practice of law that practicing law is not for the weak of heart. I have seen good lawyers leave the profession to fill vending machines. I can count on four fingers the attorneys I have met since law school that I actually liked and respected. I tell prospective attorneys the profession is as bad as everyone says. It has gotten worse over the years instead of better, and the reputation of attorneys has gone from bad to worse.

Yet, there is something about the courtroom and the smell of paper; and once an attorney, you are always an attorney. There is no escape. Even in my dreams I am an attorney screaming, "You can't do that! I'm a lawyer. I will bring a legal action against you," and when the little guy is wronged---like it or not---I end up in the courtroom doing what I love to hate, the practice of law.

Earl Warren (March 19, 1891 – July 9, 1974) was the 14th Chief Justice of the United States and was elected Governor of California three times. In the words of Chief Justice Earl Warren, "It is the spirit and not the form of law that keeps justice alive."

CHAPTER TWO

Do Attorneys All Have The Word Jerk Printed On Their Foreheads?

While I would love to say the answer to the above question is no, the truth is that most attorneys probably do have the word jerk printed on their foreheads. Now, it is not entirely their faults; and they will argue, as all attorneys *will* argue, that it is someone else's fault, that they did not do it, and that they have the utmost respect for both you and the law, which they probably don't, otherwise they would follow it. Probably the first rule of professional ethics should be, "Don't be a jerk."

That said, let's look at those rules. The rules begin with the following statement:

"The following rules are intended to regulate professional conduct of members of the State Bar through discipline. They have been adopted by the Board of Governors of the State Bar of California and approved by the

You Can't Do That!

Supreme Court of California pursuant to Business and professions Code sections 6076 and 6077 to protect the public and to promote respect and confidence in the legal profession. These rules together with any standards adopted by the Board of Governors pursuant to these rules shall be binding upon all members of the State Bar."

Following this statement there are a lot of definitions concerning who is a lawyer, what is a law firm and the purpose of the rules, just in case you don't get it. The rules specifically state the rules were established for the purpose of discipline, and authority is cited right in the rules. The rules do *not* say they were enacted to be used as a sword against your opponent. Since the Rules were enacted in furtherance of the lawful practice of law and as a guideline for attorneys by which they should abide, all attorneys should be familiar with these rules and with any subsequent changes to the rules.

Right now the rules in California are going into a bit of an overhaul, mainly with the use of the language in the rules to make them more like the rules adopted in other states, and you can read all about the current and former rules on the State Bar website at http://rules.calbar.ca.gov/Rules/RulesofProfessionalConduct/CurrentRules/Rule1100.asp.

The bar begins its discussion of the rules with " Professional Integrity In General," in Chapter One. This is a very important rule section because my experience has been that some attorneys just do not seem to understand exactly what professional integrity is. So

You Can't Do That!

what is professional integrity? Well, the rules do not *exactly* say in and of themselves what professional integrity is, but instead refers attorneys to Business and Professions Code sections 6076 and 6077 "to protect the public and to promote respect and confidence in the legal profession." Oh yes, and the current Rules of Professional Conduct also say you can still refer to them as the Rules of Professional Responsibility, which to me means a bit more---responsibility trumping conduct any day of the week in my mind. Because to me, part of the problem with attorneys is they do not take responsibility for their actions; and perhaps that is a reflection of our society in general.

What then does Business and Professions Code sections 6076 and 6077 say? I looked it up just to make sure, and you should look it up too. California Business Code Section 6076 says: "With the approval of the Supreme Court, the Board of Governors may formulate and enforce rules of professional conduct for all members of the bar in the State." Section 6077 says, "The rules of professional conduct adopted by the board, when approved by the Supreme Court, are binding upon all members of the State Bar.

For a willful breach of any of these rules, "the board has power to discipline members of the State Bar by reproval, public or private, or to recommend to the Supreme Court the suspension from practice for a period not exceeding three years of members of the State Bar."

You Can't Do That!

Now I was trying to find the word integrity and its definition in all of that, but it wasn't there. Perhaps this is the problem. Attorneys do not know the meaning of the word "integrity." What exactly does the word "integrity" mean?

The Merriam-Webster dictionary defines integrity as:

1: firm adherence to a code of especially moral or artistic values : INCORRUPTIBILITY
2: an unimpaired condition : SOUNDNESS
3: the QUALITY or state of being complete or undivided : COMPLETENESS

It gives examples of integrity:

1. He's a man of the highest *integrity*.
2. I admire her artistic *integrity*.
3. She had the *integrity* to refuse to compromise on matters of principle.
4. Without music, the film loses its *integrity*.
5. They are trying to preserve the cultural *integrity* of the community.
6. The EARTHQUAKE may have damaged the building's structural *integrity*.

See: http://www.merriam-webster.com/dictionary/integrity

It therefore stands to reason that attorneys are supposed to adhere to a strict code of moral responsibility, and they are supposed to be incorruptible. Our condition as counsels of record are to be unimpaired, complete and incorruptible, undivided and sound. And while no man is perfect in any moral way; and while no man is without sin, attorneys should strive to accomplish the singular goal of being a person of integrity, not a damaged version of a building struck by earthquake. Integrity? It all sounds lovely, but this is rarely

You Can't Do That!

what we find out there in the real world. And that, my friends, is merely the beginning of this discussion as this chapter only briefly discusses rule 1-100 of the California Rules of professional conduct.

Chapter Three

Moving Onward And Upward

Now, let's look at the rules in a sort of partial overview manner, stopping along the way at points of interest. From Rule 1-100, you would think we would logically go to Rule 1-101. Instead, the rules illogically move forward with Rule 1-110, and that rule basically says we must comply with any public or private reproval for not following the rules. The next rule in the chapter is Rule 1-120 and states "A member shall not knowingly assist in, solicit, or induce any violation of these rules or the State Bar Act." (This should be a given.) Next comes Rule 1-200 and that basically says you should not make any false statements, etc. to become a member of the California State Bar for either admission to the state bar or readmission to the state bar.

You Can't Do That!

Why the rules skip around like they do is anyone's best guess. Perhaps at one time there were more rules. I am not inclined to do any research on that subject, however.

Rule 1-300 states there shall be no authorized practice of law, and you should not practice law in a jurisdiction where you are not authorized to practice law. This rule seems like a given,

Rule 1-310 states, "A member shall not form a partnership with a person who is not a lawyer if any of the activities of that partnership consist of the practice of law." This rule also seems pretty clear. So do not partner with an accountant or a guy who chases ambulances and share your fees with them. You can, of course, hire an accountant, just don't practice law with an accountant or give them a stake in the outcome of a case or you may be accused of forming a partnership with him. Hire him. Have him send you a bill. Pay the bill. Do not hire anyone to chase ambulances at all. (But you know that, right?)

Rule 1-311 says the employment of disbarred, suspended, resigned, or involuntarily inactive member is prohibited.

The rules offer the following legal authority to define what constitutes the practice of law: "*Farnham v. State Bar* (1976) 17 Cal.3d 605 [131 Cal.Rptr. 611]; *Bluestein v. State Bar* (1974) 13 Cal.3d 162 [118 Cal.Rptr. 175]; *Baronv. City of Los Angeles* (1970) 2 Cal.3d 535 [86Cal.Rptr. 673]; *Crawford v. State Bar* (1960) 54 Cal.2d 659 [7 Cal.Rptr. 746]; *People v. Merchants Protective*

You Can't Do That!

Corporation (1922) 189 Cal. Rule-310 531, 535 [209 P. 363]; *People v. Landlords Professional Services* (1989) 215 Cal.App.3d 1599 [264 Cal.Rptr.548]; and *People v. Sipper* (1943) 61 Cal.App.2d Supp. 844 [142 P.2d 960]."

Rule 1-320 states neither a member of the bar nor a law firm shall directly or indirectly share legal fees with a person who is not a lawyer; and this goes along (sort of) with Rule 1-310. Or maybe it was written to reinforce the issue. After that, there is a lot of discussion in the rules and more rules pertaining to advertisement, and what you can and cannot say and how to conduct yourself as an attorney when you are advertising your wares as counsel. The main thing you should always remember is your disclaimer. My disclaimer can be read at the beginning of this book. I am going to be telling you a lot of stuff in this book, but of course it is not meant to give specific advice on any area of the law. For specific advice on any area of the law you should consult your attorney. Oh yes, and when you send emails and faxes you should always put in a disclaimer as well, stating the information contained is personal and confidential, intended only for the recipient, may be attorney client or attorney work product privileged and if received in error notify sender immediately and return, delete or destroy. And be careful what you say because any offhanded remark by a lawyer may be considered legal advice. Even though you are the smartest attorney in the world, just smile at that cocktail party or barbeque when you

You Can't Do That!

are asked for any opinion on the law and tell them, "You better ask your attorney." If the response is, "I thought you were my attorney," tell them to make an appointment to see you in your office. Why? Because even if they do not retain you, if they follow your off-handed advice and something---anything---goes wrong they will turn around and sue you for all you are worth.

And now venturing even further off the subject, your current clients can do the same thing. I represented someone in an arbitration over a property issue. I told this person she should file a claim with her homeowners insurance, and she did not want to do this. (I had called her insurance and asked if she was covered and was told she wasn't; but I advised her to file a claim anyway.) She did not want her premium to go up and thought I would be less expensive in the long run. This woman sent me cards telling me how wonderful I was. We went to the arbitration, and when she broke even and didn't make her windfall profit, she sought out another counsel who, of course, immediately called me and *threatened* to sue me for malpractice and report me to the state bar (which you are not supposed to do) for not calling and/or advising a homeowner's claim. Then I was faced with an attorney/client privilege issue—but since she had raised the issue and hired this other attorney to get me, I was free to defend myself with the caveat that my former client was raising this issue, and the information was otherwise privileged. And yes, you must state this, or you should. Luckily, I took notes, kept a phone record file, and the insurance company also kept a record of the call. I told the other counsel this and referred him to the insurer. That was the end of that. Did I tell you this woman was supposedly a friend of mine? The bottom line is do not trust anyone. Everyone lies, and if you are incapable of lying like I am, then you need to keep good notes and good records. It pays. Assume nothing. Confirm everything. (I ended up reducing my attorney fees. The reason this woman, my friend, did this was she just did not want to pay me my bill in full.) The sad part was the attorney was ready to accuse me of malpractice before confirming the facts, a breach of *his* professional responsibility. The woman has not spoken to me since, in spite of all the lovely cards saying how wonderful I was. I guess this is why one should also not get talked into representing family and friends, although I must confess this *is* actually why I got into this business. Oops!

This is another reason when I dream, I scream, "You can't do that! I am a lawyer!" People can and will do just about everything and anything; and while I sympathize with the need to survive in this world, I do not condone *not* taking responsibility for one's wrongs! You see, it isn't *only* lawyers who need a lesson in integrity! This is why we have rules and laws; and this is why we need them, even if they are rarely followed, are interpreted to death, and drive you crazy as a person of morality, assuming you are one. In fact, I am so convinced that one should take responsibility for one's wrongs, I even wrote a children's book (which shall remain nameless) on the subject. Perhaps if we start with the very young, we *can* make a difference in this world. If everyone lit just one little candle, what a bright, bright world this would be.

Chapter Four
The Blind Really Can Lead You

One of the four attorneys I have actually liked and admired in this business was my mentor and friend, the late Bob Deems, who happened to also be an attorney who was blind. We met when I was first practicing law, and he is why I do know absolutely that the profession used to be a gentlemen's profession and was not *always* the cut-throat way it is today.

Bob and I met as opposite counsel on a child support case, which I usually do not do, but in this case I was glad I did because I met Bob. I remember that when we began the case he gave me a very hard time, but later told me he always began that way to test the other counsel; and he decided I was okay. I forgot to dot an" I" or some other trivial matter on a contempt filing against his client; and because contempt was a criminal charge, Bob pointed out to the court that it was not a trivial matter as I had suggested and that I

You Can't Do That!

should be held to the highest standard on this, no less than he would expect from himself---and he was absolutely right. I continued undaunted, however.

The contempt filing was as a result of non-payment of child support and an effort to get a wage garnishment. Once the judge gave us the garnishment we weren't interested in the contempt issue, because we really didn't want the guy in jail because he couldn't exactly work from jail. Now, what I *learned* from Bob was what integrity within the meaning of professionally responsibility and vigorous representation of your client actually meant.

We stood and argued how much child support should be awarded, and somehow in the back and forth and input from the judge got to something like a three dollar a month difference in my favor between the two of us. After another twenty minutes or so of back and forth legal argument (and we were having an absolutely great time, by the way) my client tugged on my sleeve and whispered she really wasn't interested in the three dollars a month difference. I looked at Bob and said, "Are we really going to continue to argue over an extra three dollars a month?" Bob looked at the judge, said "Yes;" and then explained that over a year those three dollars a month added up to thirty six dollars and over 10 years it grew to $360 dollars. Bob said he would continue to argue for it, not to mention the accrued interest on the money that would also add to the totals if the money was put into a savings account.

18

You Can't Do That!

My client looked at me and said, "Give him the three dollars," and laughed.

I said, "You can have the three dollars a month," and the judge smiled.

The judge later told Bob he had never had such a good time in the courtroom, and that he didn't even care if we went over our allotted time estimation and cause him to miss half of his lunch hour.

Bob and I were best of friends after that day. If I had a question regarding ethics or any area of the law, I went straight to Bob for a second opinion. Of course, we never named names or revealed confidences or privileged matters, but it was good for me as a solo practitioner to have someone to go to court for me if I was sick and someone to call when I needed advice on something. I ended up going to court for Bob as well when he was ill, and when he died, I felt a great, great loss. You know, sometimes he would just call me to tell me a good joke because he felt I could use some cheering up for the day---and usually he was right! Practicing law is not only *not* for the weak of heart, it is also *not* for the faint of heart.

Bob could see better than anyone I ever knew, even if he was blind; and the point is, make a friend if you can out there, someone who can be used as a sounding board when you have a legal or ethical question. Bob was my standard for what a lawyer should be. He never made a lot of money, but he did have a moral and ethical career. He taught me how to stay out of the soup as well as the

You Can't Do That!

meaning of true integrity. I also knew if we were ever on opposite sides of the table again, he would fight me tooth and nail; and he knew I would do the exact same thing. . . having been there and done that and having found a mutual respect as attorneys for one another that we really couldn't find anywhere else. It is also where I learned the law did not *have to be* the way it was and where I got the courage to really stand up and fight no matter what, because no matter how hard I felt I was working to defend what was right, just and good, I knew Bob was fighting even harder. I also learned what it was *really* like to be blind, but that is another story that won't be told here. I know what it is like to be blind, because Bob told me. I didn't ask. He just told me. You have to work even harder.

Vigorous advocacy of your client does not meaning throwing your opposition under the bus, and it *does mean* doing the right thing for everyone. Doing the right thing is more work, but it *can* be done. You just have to revise your way of thinking and erase the word jerk off of your forehead.

Chapter Five
The Nitty Gritty

Now that I have diverted in order to explain how you can form an opinion about what integrity is, or at least how I formed my opinion as to what it is, we will go back to our overview discussion of the California Rules of Professional Conduct, aka The California Rules of Professional Responsibility. Basically, the more you read the rules the better you will know them, so I will refer you to the website URL where you can read them for yourself and even download them. In fact, if you are caught making a mistake, you may have to pass a test on them in order to regain or continue your right to practice law. Therefore, you need to read the rules and know them. http://rules.calbar.ca.gov/Rules/RulesofProfessionalConduct.aspx

Rule 1-500 states "A member shall not be a party to or participate in offering or making an agreement, whether in connection with the settlement of a lawsuit or otherwise, if the agreement restricts the right of a member to practice law. . ."

Now you would think this rule is rarely violated, right? Wrong. And yes, this law has been used against me. I was serving as a voluntary counsel for a non-profit booster club for a swim team where my daughter was a member and my husband was the president of the board, something I now avoid like the plague. It seems I have a difficult time getting into any case or anything without uncovering a huge fraud, or worse, behind what appears to be something simple and benign. To make a very long story short, I uncovered a situation where two coaches did not have coaches cards (which immediately voided all insurance and removed sanctions from meets they attended (which were all the swim meets) and who were... oh yes, did I tell you? They were child molesters. They were fired by the board when they left a group of pre-teen girls alone on a military base (against the rules) with Navy Seals—the alpha males—in excess of fifteen minutes, and that was when I was called in to look at things after the fact.

Not only did I discover this problem, but I also discovered the treasurer had embezzled funds from the team in excess of what appeared to be fifty thousand dollars. The two child molesters (one of which admitted to a later incident involving a child under the age of fourteen and served time) hijacked the swim team, or part of it, and tried to do a take-over of the team, all allowed by USA

You Can't Do That!

Swimming and the local swim association. Our group formed a new swim team and a new booster club and still contended we were the other team in reality, because the bylaws were not followed in the takeover. Not only did USA swimming side with the bad guys, they said they were more upset with me than they were with the coaches, and a local attorney representing the local swim association violated law 1-500 by banning me from representing another swim team in USA swimming for a period of three years, which pretty much did away with my standing (or so they thought) to bring a lawsuit against the wrongdoers. It is true. It happened. I wrote a book about it. It was my first book, "Everything You Never Wanted Tto Know About Your Nonprofit Corporation."

Now it wasn't as though I was dying to represent a swim team or anything like that. It was just that I was trying to do the right thing. And I pointed out this violation of the code of professional ethics to the attorney and to the attorney for USA Swimming in my defense appeal from this quasi-judicial order and was ignored. Meanwhile, the EDD and the IRS were coming around because withholding amounts had not been paid by the embezzling treasurer, and a former employee of the team booster club called me and said there was no record of his employment on his social security information letter. (Actually, I believe when the former employee called me, he asked me to call the IRS and find out why there was no record of his employment, all before the team takeover; and then everything just started happening.) Initially, all I wanted was for the treasurer to give us the books so we could make arrangements with the IRS and the EDD to pay them what they were owed---that. plus the coach thing, caused the uproar.

The bottom line is you are not supposed to do this, and in my opinion not doing a proper investigation of these guys, and all of them, was a dereliction of duty. Oh yes, I also discovered the booster team had its corporate status suspended, and they were legally not allow to conduct business as a corporation in the State of California; and that the local branch of USA Swimming had its corporation status also suspended, and the national governing body of USA Swimming was *not* registered in the State of California as a foreign corporation doing business in the state. (They claimed there was jurisdiction over me through them when they had no jurisdiction over me or any actual jurisdiction in the state. I wasn't even a member of USA Swimming.) Three years later, a twelve year old child had her life ruined by one of the child molesting coaches. Recently, broad allegations of child molesting up to the highest levels have come out against USA swimming; and USA Swimming is now registered in all fifty states as a foreign corporation. I was also fined $350 when I tried to appeal the local decision for refusing to be quiet about the child molestation and I had to pay $300 to file the appeal! The decision to limit my practice of law was upheld by USA Swimming. I tried to explain in my papers, as I said, that this was wrong; but it wasn't a settlement agreement, it was an order by an administrative body in a quasi judicial decision written by a California attorney in an effort to resolve the matters I raised with the local and thereafter the national association, which leads me to believe there was no authority to do this, and it was more likely than not violating the rule against limiting the practice of counsel. After all, it came after a threat by opposing counsel they would do *anything* to stop me, and they basically attempted to prevent me (as I felt bound to obey this ruling) from filing a civil action to get further resolve in the California Superior Court. (More will be said on that later.) I decided not to report it to the State Bar, because the attorney who engaged in the decision to limit my law practice was retiring, had cancer and was probably going to die. Also, as I recall, I did get limited right from the national body, in the end, to file a civil action, which my clients collectively decided not to do. Besides, I didn't need this grief over something I had volunteered to do. But I was very sad for the children, and I am very sorry that it hurt my own child's swimming career---but she did go to the 10K Olympic Trials anyway! And she went there unmolested.

By the way, I have asked for (on more than one occasion) and *never* received an apology from the local swim association or from from USA swimming; and I can tell you from my own experience that when they say they promptly investigate all allegations of child molestation, they are not being entirely truthful, to say the least.

You Can't Do That!

These people made my life absolutely miserable, and I was only trying to do what was right and good; and like my old friend, Bob, I was representing my clients vigorously.

The two child molesting coaches? One is coaching at a local community college. (At least those girls are the age of majority.) The other is coaching (according to my sources) a water polo team in Mexico (to where he was deported—on probation with the caveat he never coach children again). And how did I know they were child molesters? One of the high schools where one of the coaches coached let him go because of an inappropriate sexual relationship with a minor, a fourteen year old girl on the swim team. All I had to do was call the school principal to confirm the allegation. The other guy? Someone came to me and said she took her daughter off our swim team because he was calling her and asking her to go on a date with him. The mother told him to date someone his own age. The girl was twelve years old.

None of this was good enough for USA Swimming, even with proof. The mother of the high school girl who was fourteen did not want to press charges. He got away with it. No conviction? They would not act. Oh, as I recall, the child molesters who did not have coaches cards *were* suspended---one for 30 days, the other for 45 days, a pittance compared to not allowing me to volunteer and not to practice law representing any swim team or swimmer, or even to sell a hot dog to help earn money for my child's swim team for three years, my husband for two--And these coaches were coaching without coaches cards---one of them for six years! And no coaches cards voided all the USA swim liability insurance wherever they were---even at swim meets, both in town and out of town!

And the embezzler? She was prevented from volunteering to be a treasurer for a swim team. She also hired legal counsel who threatened me, had someone report me to the California State Bar Association (more on that later) and used the entire process to attempt to prevent me from going beyond the administrative hearing stages into an action in the Superior Court (as I said). My health went to pot, and I became physically ill. What was going to happen to the children? I didn't want to be right, but I was---about everything---and the *worst* thing is a child was hurt, a beautiful innocent child was hurt. And, Oh yes, I forgot, for the next two years the USA local swim organizations gave these two coaches the honor of coaching the 12-14 year old girls at zones—a stay in a hotel in a place far away from Mom and Dad.

Winning at any cost is wrong. At least follow the rules.

Chapter Six
About Communications

Rule 1-700 says in part, "While representing a client, a member shall not communicate directly or indirectly about the subject of the representation with a party the member knows to be represented by another lawyer in the matter, unless the member has the consent of the other lawyer."

This means you should take absolutely no chances. If someone calls you on the phone from the other side just to talk, and if you have not heard from an opposing counsel, ask if they are represented by counsel. Even if they say no, get it in writing from them or do not talk to them. I had an ethics professor in law school who insisted everyone lied. He said even our clients would lie to us, and to trust no one. Being a person who is incapable of lying I do not see the purpose of lying. I always worried about the angel on my own shoulder telling me to do good and the devil on the other shoulder telling me to do bad when I was a kid. My mother, who is a minor exaggerator of the truth, had me convinced I would burn in hell if I told a lie or did something bad. For me it stuck, even when I found out my own mother was less than truthful, I could not lie. I cheated once in algebra in high school and have felt guilty ever since. That's me. I am solid. I always try to do the right thing. But that is also why I am passionate about the legal ethics of the law. It makes me very sad that my ethics professor was probably right.

Even Bob told me to get everything in writing, and if I had to talk to someone, to insist on either recording the conversation or to memorialize it in writing. It has served me well, this advice, because I have even had counsel try to skirt out of an agreed to settlement. The recording I made saved me the time of having to make a motion to enforce the settlement when he insisted the agreement was other than it actually was. And, yes, I told opposing counsel I was recording him during the settlement discussions. He just forgot. Since Bob was blind, he recorded everything because he couldn't take notes. It was assumed he was recording, so he didn't have to tell anyone, but he did anyway.

Of course, when you only communicate in writing they will tear that apart as well; and even the kindest letter to the opposition will be incorrectly labeled a threat. Again, you must be careful.

Do not tell your client to call the client of the opposing counsel, because this is an indirect communication with someone

You Can't Do That!

represented by counsel. Do not shout from the rooftop something you want the client of an opposing counsel to know. If you have anything to say or an offer to give, then make it official. Make a settlement offer. That has to be communicated to the opposing attorney's client under the rules. Watch everything you do and say. It is true. It is as bad as you think. You can trust no one.

The only way you can really talk to a person represented by counsel is if they are seeking a second opinion and you have no conflict of interest and do not represent the adverse party, or if they have fired counsel and are seeking to establish a contract with you for representation and you do not represent the opposing party. You can also talk to the parties together if you are merely affirming an agreement made between the parties outside litigation where only your client is represented, and where you advise and state in the agreement that the agreement was reached independently and that you advised the other party to seek independent counsel and he or she did not desire to do so. Additionally, you can reach an agreement outside the courtroom door and giving the same advice, present that agreement as a stipulation before the court with the above caveat and put it on the record, thereafter preparing the document for signing and filing, as entered before the court, and filing it. The judge may even inquire if the other party was advised to seek the advice of his own counsel, so you better have advised it; and you will be out of luck if he or she says no---but at least that is one thing that has never happened to me. It is hard to believe, but it is true. I think I have had just about everything else possible happen to me, but at least not that. That is a sad statement when you stop to think lay people may be more morally structured than many of us in the legal profession. Being an attorney who cannot lie may be a disadvantage to me as well as my compulsion to do what is right at any cost, but I would not have it any other way. It is who I am, just like all of you are who you are. I have to be me, and you have to be you.

CHAPTER SEVEN
Can You Keep A Secret?

If you can't keep a secret then you shouldn't be an attorney because as an attorney you are charged with keeping the confidentiality of your client under Rule 3-100. This rule was written and adopted so that an attorney would be required under Business and Professions Code section 6068, subdivision (e)(1), which provides it is a duty of a member of the State Bar of California ". . .to maintain inviolate the confidence, and at every peril to himself or herself to preserve the secrets, of his or her client."

Now you would not think an attorney would try to use *that* particular rule to gain an advantage in the case about which I just spoke, the embezzler and the two child molesters case, would you? But *yes*, an attorney did just that. In a somewhat twisted mind the attorney kept insisting that the swim team he wrestled away with the embezzler and the child molesters and hijacked by calling an unauthorized (under the terms of the bylaws) election to do away with a board striving to protect children from people who were nothing more than criminals preying on children---that somehow I was or had been *their* attorney because they were *really* the swim team, and the people on the board I represented were not. And in this delusion he kept threatening me saying I was not only violating confidences, I was also guilty of breaking Rule 3-310 Avoiding the Representation of Adverse Interests and would report me to the State bar. Nothing could be further from the truth, and this attorney was, in fact, in my opinion (and I did tell him this in writing) advising the violation of law. (I did not mention Rule 3-210.) He was not directing the embezzler to return funds, he blocked the team bank account allowing only the embezzler access to it, requiring me to advise the bank to hold all the money until the matter could be resolved because there was a question of ownership, and he further (after being told this had been done) allowed one of the child molesters to secure water (a pool) using the identity of my husband, who was president of the board, and also allowed someone to represent to the IRS that he was my husband. When called on this, the attorney shouted, "We had to! We didn't have access to those records; and we couldn't get water!." Now it seems to me that this attorney was not only advising the violation of law, but he was also a part of breaking the law. Furthermore, after a period of time the bank sent all the money in the account to a team PO Box under the exclusive control of the embezzler, which they eventually got after a series of legal filings with the postal service where no one would listen to me when I said all the money left in that account needed to go to the EDD and/or the IRS to pay down all the money owed there that was embezzled by the former treasurer that this attorney represented. What the attorney told the local branch of USA Swimming was that they needed the money to pay the coaches---TO PAY THE CHILD MOLESTERS WHO HAD BEEN FIRED AND WHO WITH THE EMBEZZLING TREASUER TOOK OVER THE SWIM TEAM!!! Oh yes, and they did this with parents the one child molester brought with him when he took kids with him from another team when my board hired him. He had been with us for less than a year.

One thing about child molesters is that they are extremely charming and endearing, but legal counsel should know better. A win of any kind is not worth exposing even a single child to danger. And nothing is worth doing or risking that. But I was shouting at the wind—and yes, while a possible court action against them was indeed pending, that attorney advised someone that I will call a stooge to file his complaint against me with the bar stating in part that I was representing an adverse interest to my client, who was supposedly these child molesters and the embezzler. Now it didn't hold, but I had to respond. (And there is even more.)

You Can't Do That!

The bottom line is there are those out there who will do anything. There are those who will break the rules and use the rules to break the rules, and there comes a point where you just know that. In fact when I researched this counsel I found out this was not the first time he had done this to gain a legal advantage in a pending action. The attorney prior to me did bring an action against him and did win it, but that guy is still out there as far as I know, blissfully practicing law not even caring that a child was molested three years later. In the hearing, even in the face of evidence to the contrary over certain things that had happened that I set before everyone in the papers—no one would call the school district or the principal, no one would believe inappropriate comments were sent in emails, even with the evidence before them. And so these guys continued and now continue to harm children.

This is why I scream in my dreams, "You can't do that!"

I never represented this threesome. I uncovered their crimes. Opposing counsel and USA Swimming allowed them to continue. I was a lowly volunteer. I got nothing for my trouble. I was pro bono counsel. All I wanted was to help the children and to do the right thing. They finally believe me, the parents who believed them; but unfortunately it is too late. The system failed. We tried everything, even going to the city. No one would listen. No one would take these coaches off the deck. The embezzler became an afterthought in comparison. She only stole $50,000.00. That was nothing in comparison to stealing a child's innocence.

The point of all of this is follow the rules and do not wrongly use the rules by making threats to gain an advantage in a pending action. You still have to live with yourself and what you have done, and in the end God and/or karma is sure to get you and bite you in the foot. What goes around eventually comes around.

Of course, this is only the opinion of one attorney and for specific advice on any area of the law, you do need to contact your own independent counsel. I may not always know what the hell I am talking about (according to yet another one of my law school professors) but I do defend with vigorous advocacy.(Actually, he said I do it beautifully.) No one is perfect, but shouldn't we at least try to be perfect?

Chapter Eight
What Are You Going To Do About It?

There is one rule I know for sure was broken by someone I highly respect as a lawyer. I would say it couldn't be proven, but since a child resulted from it, it can be proven. Nevertheless, it happened to a friend, I consider it none of my business and none of the direct parties concerned made a complaint about it. You, on the other hand may not be so lucky. What is that rule? It is Rule 3-120, Sexual Relations With Client. Do not have sexual relations with a client. You might get caught in the copy room. You could get in trouble. A rejected lover may stalk you, or worse yet report you to the state bar. Don't do it. And that is enough said about that subject for now, and I will not go into the definitions of what sexual relations are. (Bill Clinton wore that discussion pretty much to death.)

You Can't Do That!

If you do not carry liability insurance then under the rules you must disclose the fact. It doesn't matter if we are being insured to death or if you think you can take care of yourself. The state bar mandates you have the right to make the decision about whether you carry liability insurance, but you do not have the right (in nearly all instances) not to tell your client or prospective client (before he or she signs on the dotted line) that you do not have it.

Rule 3-410 Disclosure of Professional Liability Insurance provides in part as follows: "A member who knows or should know that he or she does not have professional liability insurance shall inform a client in writing, at the time of the client's engagement of the member, that the member does not have professional liability insurance whenever it is reasonably foreseeable that the total amount of the member's legal representation of the client in the matter will exceed four hours."

Look up the rule to read all the definitions and ins and outs for yourself, but the bottom line is if they decide to sue you and you don't have it, then besides losing the shirt off your back, you could lose your right to practice law and then you couldn't by another shirt. Maybe you could get off with a public or private reproval or something, but this is such an easy thing to do, why not just do it? Save yourself the grief.

The rules say that all you have to do is put this at the end of your contract, *"Pursuant to California Rule of Professional Conduct*

3-410, I am informing you in writing that I do not have professional liability insurance." Or if you like, you can have the client sign separate agreement that just says that. It's very easy, so just do it. If you stop carrying liability insurance then you must send your client this statement, *"Pursuant to California Rule of Professional Conduct 3-410, I am informing you in writing that I no longer have professional liability insurance."*

That said, Rule 3-400--Limiting Liability to Client, does not allow you to contractually limit your liability to a client so if you aren't willing to take the risk that you just may be wrong, do not take the case. Do not take a case for which you do not have the knowledge and capability to handle and for which you do not expect to attain the knowledge, expertise and capability to handle with competence. No one can know everything; and besides, opposing counsel will be very happy to point out your alleged incompetence to you, trust me on that. It is a mantra used to shake your confidence even when you absolutely know what you are doing and have the law behind you to prove it. Rule 3-110 Failing to Act Competently states that a member (of the state bar) shall not intentionally, recklessly, or repeatedly fail to perform legal services with competence. Rest assured more times than not those who will threaten you with the rules will be sure to say you are not acting with competence, even if you are acting pro bono and even if you are not getting paid a single cent and are doing whatever you are doing out of the goodness of

You Can't Do That!

your heart. Please do not let this daunt you. Doing the right thing is always good. Ask Hollywood. Good always seems to come out ahead in the old time movies. Could life possibly have been so good and simple then?

After working for what seems like forever on a case you get an offer of settlement. It is a low ball offer. What do you do? Rule 3-510 Communication of Settlement Offer—provides that you must immediately inform your client of all the terms and conditions of any offer made in a criminal matter, and all amounts, terms, and conditions of any written offer of settlement made to the client in all other matters. It also provides that any oral offers of settlement made to the client in a civil matter should be communicated if they are "significant" for the purposes of rule 3-500.

The bottom line is should probably report all offers of settlement to your client, because if you go to trial and lose and the client discovers there was an offer out there that would have given them any advantage, even in the limiting of fees paid to you, they will most certainly argue the offer made was "significant," and no amount of arguing by you will convince them otherwise. On a dime the client who loves and adores you can turn like a worm---or should I say *for a dime* the client who loves and adores you *will* turn like a worm. It is not a nice world out there. You can't look at a settlement offer in relation to how much you will get out of it. You need to look at the offer from the position of your client and do and advise

You Can't Do That!

what is best for your client, not what is best for you. If you are working on a contingency, and the offer is a low ball and your client accepts it, bite the bullet. It is not about you. It is all about your client and what is best for your client. Just make sure the client is informed in writing that he or she is accepting or entering into an offer against the advice of counsel. Sometimes, after accepting an offer and your careful communication of it, a client will tell you they changed their mind and that they want to go back for more; so you need to also make it very clear when they accept an offer *that* is the last piece of the pie they will get. Your client needs to understand once the bell is rung, it cannot be unrung. If they don't fully understand this, and if you do not get this in writing from your client, it could come back to bite you, and once again---your client could report you to the state bar and/or they will get some unscrupulous attorney (and of these there are many) to accuse you of malpractice, especially if the client owes you some money and this was not a contingency case. When it comes to money, people *will do* just about anything. Once a client even asked me to give up my statutory 12% on a worker's compensation case where he had received a substantial amount of money and training, and he had blown all the money. Trust no one. Follow the rules. Protect yourself. Even that is sometimes just not enough. There is an old saying that sometimes things have to get worse before they can get better. Maybe this is the worse.

Chapter Nine
Other Important Stuff

There is a bunch of other stuff in the rules of which you should be aware. And there is a bunch of stuff you need to know that really isn't set forth in the rules. To begin with, when I set out to write this book I discovered how woefully inadequate the rules are, and this is probably why they are so easily broken. Television and mass media have set about to create a sort of cult admiration for those who break the rules. Government bails out the banks which appear to be rife with borderline, criminal activity. I called out Enron and told my husband before they fell, and a company counsel that I fondly referred to (behind the scenes in the hot tub as Mr. Malpractice) said "Oh no, Ken Lay is a good guy." My husband's company had a contract for energy that was set at a limit that was supposed to lapse if the rates went down, and Enron was refusing to honor the contract and release its rights to provide the company energy. It didn't take a rocket scientist to figure that one out. The question is how many attorneys at Enron failed to properly advise Mr. Lay and others that what they were doing was wrong? Where were the regulatory agencies? Oh that's right, they were gone. They were a part of the movement of deregulation that included our banking industry. How well that one worked out for us all. Not. When will attorneys become true advocate and fight for that three dollars a month like my friend Bob did that day in court? Practicing law should be about doing the right thing. Hmmmm. . . now what is that oath we say when we are admitted to the practice of law?

CALIFORNIA BUSINESS AND PROFESSIONS CODE

"6067. Oath. Every person on his admission shall take an oath to support the Constitution of the United States and the Constitution of the State of California, and faithfully to discharge the duties of any attorney at law to the best of his knowledge and ability. A certificate of the oath shall be indorsed upon his license. (Added by Stats. 1939, c 34. p. 354, Sec. 1.)"

Ironically, there are no attorneys actually licensed in California. If you ask, none can produce a certificate. An attorney can only produce his or her bar membership card privately issued by the California State Bar Association and a letter of acknowledgement from the state supreme court.

Rule 5-200 Trial Conduct states that in presenting a matter to a tribunal, a member (an attorney) shall employ, for the purpose of

You Can't Do That!

maintaining the causes confided to the member such means only as are consistent with truth. Now the question is do the words "consistent with the truth" mean something different from telling the truth? Can you represent anything you like as long as you don't mention something inconsistent with the truth? The rule also says you should not seek to mislead the judge, judicial officer, or jury by an artifice or false statement of fact or law and you should (shall) not assert personal knowledge of the facts at issue, except when testifying as a witness. And this is why opposing counsel, if they see you as a threat to them, will try to turn you into a witness on your own case. They want to get rid of you, and they will again use the rules of professional responsibility against you even as you vehemently argue work product and attorney/client privilege. I know, this also happened to me.

You ask how you can become a witness? One trick that can be used against you is to wrongfully accuse you of malpractice through pleadings—the "no one would have known there was a fraud but for the fact you told them by filing an action against them, or in my case, an action to quiet title" defense. Yes, I had the unfortunate experience of uncovering a fraudulent conveyance and began an action to quiet my client's title. This was their defense. In the process I found out title insurance was really not worth the paper on which it was written because it only insured what the insurer was unable to find in a title search and the document absolved itself from negligence as did the current law. Now it seems to me that if attorneys do title searches, and even if they oversee title searches and defend them, they should be able to see on the face of a document that an interest or a part of an interest went back to the transferor of property. In this instance a bank sold a property out of a foreclosure in which they held a multi-interest in title, business and house; and my client paid for the business he purchased sufficient amounts to satisfy all the junior lien-holders, including the EDD who came forward to attach proceeds from my client's business in the form of payments he was making to the guy who had the bank foreclose, wash junior lien holders and sell to my client, while taking a second TD interest in the property and moving his parents into the other property, putting it in the name of his brother. My client had no idea the property was in foreclosure and had been dealing with the seller and the bank prior to the bank foreclosure that washed the lien holders. The problem was had he not brought an action to quiet title, upon discovery of this conveyance, which smacked of fraud, they could bring an action to set aside these conveyances as fraudulent conveyances. Their argument was I had committed malpractice in willfully soliciting to set aside the deed of my client by bringing an action to quiet title. In a summary judgment motion I brought the judge said he would agree that since it looked like a fish and it smelled like a fish, it probably was a fish and he agreed it looked like there *was* a prima facie case of fraud, but that it wasn't *enough* to

You Can't Do That!

grant the motion for summary judgment. The State Attorney General also wrote earlier in a letter to me that he thought it was a prima facie case of fraud, An independent arbitrator point blank asked them if they actually expected me to not come forward when discovering "all of this." He told them I had no choice but to do what I did when discovering a fraud, adding something like, "What did you expect her to do?" Yet, they went on saying I willfully solicited to set aside the deed of my client and deposed me, and I could not get a protective order. My friend Bob agreed they were trying to make me a witness in my own case, and as for the title insurance company, they sided with the fraudulent transfer because, of course, they were negligent in not uncovering it, even though the law gave them protection from that. Everything then turned on what did the title insurer know and when did the title insurer know it, and were they obligated to defend title? It was all quite bizarre.

  The bottom line is I got through the deposition, and did not end up as a witness in my own case, probably because we settled; but this is yet another way the rules of professional responsibility can and will be used against you, especially if you are treading on the toes of the big guys who generally always have their way. Might does make right. They have the money to make it so. In fact I was told point blank in chambers and in front of a law in motion judge, "I don't know who is funding this case, but our client (the title insurance company) will spend whatever it takes to destroy you and your client." I took that as a threat, and that was exactly what it was. There are judges out there who can be, shall we say, improperly influenced. All I can say is what goes around eventually comes around either in this world or the next. It is time now to take hold of the reins of justice and ride that horse before it is too late. Be careful and be aware. There is nothing you can do. As I continue to say, the practice of law is neither for the weak, nor is it for the faint of heart. And that was a subject (sort of) in part of another book I wrote, "The Great American Rip Off."

There are those out there who will accuse me and have accused me of being a whiner and a complainer and who do not like my books and who write livid reviews on Amazon saying they are terrible, full of mistakes, poorly edited, etc. The truth is never welcomed by people like this. Just maybe someday the truth actually will set us all free, but I am not going to hold my breath waiting for that day. I will not be silenced by them either. It is just not my way. I do not write to make money. I write in the hope that one person will influence another person, and that person will influence another person and so on and so forth until there comes upon us some inexplicable change. That is all I hope. Besides, no book is perfect.

There are some other things in the rules that we can probably also learn from the television program "Law and Order, such as not tampering with a jury, not hiding witnesses, not suppressing evidence and the like. No one has ever accused me of that, at least,

You Can't Do That!

or tried to use that in my cases—but it does go on as well, and these are things you should also not do.

In short, before you are admitted to the California State Bar, you have to pass a course in ethics with a grade of C or better. I remember taking that course, and some things have changed since then. It is probably a very good idea that every three years we attorneys in California are required to show completion of 25 hours of CLE, including those hours in ethics. Otherwise, things might even be worse!

Chapter Ten
I couldn't Believe It Happened To Me

It happened on my way to China to conduct some business with the PRC. There I was putting my luggage into the car with my young child looking on when across the street from an empty lot a truck zoomed up my driveway nearly hitting my dog. I screamed, "Run!" and dropped my bags and ran because I thought someone was going to take out a gun and unload it on me. A process server, that I had actually used and never used again, threw a document out the window and yelled, "You are served!"

There I was on my way to China, having given notice to opposing counsel and the court and all of the world that I was going to be gone and out of country, being served for malicious prosecution on a cause of action I had stipulated with opposing counsel before a referee to dismiss—when the underlying case was still pending. I was told later by the process server he was paid $400 just to scare me, and he did.

On the way to China I was busy calling my carrier to defend me and calling my client. He was named in the complaint, and the complaint alleged that I had committed malpractice in willfully soliciting to set aside the deed of my client by bringing an action to quiet title (one of the causes of action named in the complaint). The cause of action dismissed was a RICO cause of action, and I stipulated to dismissal at the behest of the referee I got appointed by the court during a seven day deposition of my client where he was asked the same questions over and over and over again.

Now, anyone who knows a fig about the law knows this would not stand. But after paying $2500 on a deductible, the attorney assigned by my liability policy carrier stipulated to a dismissal without my permission that prohibited me from bringing any kind of action against the title insurer and its client—yes, this was the same fraudulent conveyance case. And yes, my friend Bob agreed the insurer's attorney had just committed malpractice and offered to bring an action against the carrier for me. It was beginning to look like litigation out of control. In the end in a plea on another matter before the court I stated what had been going on, and the judge took the opposition into chambers. When he came out he put on the record that he had just been told that the opposing council had stated they would do anything to get me off the case. Then the judge countered that he was bringing his own motion before the court, and that they needed to state why he should not report them to the state bar and sanction them in excess of $3,500. He set a hearing. At the hearing the old counsel was out and as my friend, Bob said, "in came the silk suit," an attorney from the sixth largest law firm in the United States. I now had three sets of counsel to fight---all with their own discovery, during the time before discovery was limited by statute. There was the attorney for the seller and his firm, the attorney for the bank and its law firm and now the silk suits. The long and the short of it was that the attorney who brought the ill fated malicious prosecution action was out, and no sanctions were filed. The truth was he remained behind the scenes, exclusively employed by the title insurer—which was, after all, a misrepresentation before the court and me and my client that he was gone. Nothing was done. He got away with it, even though I had to deal long distance by fax with my liability carrier while in China as I negotiated contracts, got little sleep, and became as nervous as a wreck. I did enjoy the respite of shopping in Hong Kong before I came home, however.

The offending counsel was in violation of Rule 3-200 Prohibited Objectives of Employment because he brought an action, allegedly at the behest of his client, conducted a defense, asserted a position in litigation without probable cause and for the purpose of

You Can't Do That!

harassing or maliciously injuring a person. Nothing happened. He was removed from view, and the guy in the silk suit misrepresented to the court that the other guy who was set up for the hearing was no longer involved in the case. Yes, he was violating the rule regarding the misleading of the court, but so many rules were broken at this point that I was the only one counting. I could not stop it by telling them they were violating the rules of conduct, because then I would be in violation of Rule 5-100. threatening criminal, administrative, or disciplinary charges while an underlying action was pending. (At least that is what the state bar told me the other side would say whether I filed a complaint while the action was pending or confronted them, and this is why I implored the court to invoke some sanity over the matter without mentioning that advice. Now maybe that advice was a bit misguided and I should have filed a complaint anyway, but the truth is you do not want to unnecessarily anger someone with whom you are trying to reach resolve. That, in my meager opinion, simply makes matters worse.

The proposed changes to this rule will now make the rule more specific and understandable. It will say if approved by the California Supreme Court that the rule "does not apply to a threat to bring a civil action. It also does not prohibit actually presenting criminal, administrative, or disciplinary charges, even if doing so creates an advantage in a civil dispute."

See: PROPOSED RULES OF PROFESSIONAL CONDUCT

You Can't Do That!

(Adopted by the Board of Governors on July 24, 2010 and September 22, 2010. Rules of Professional Conduct must be approved by the Supreme Court of California in order to become operative. These rules have not been approved by the Supreme Court.)

So how did I know the other guy was still out there and involved in this case? I knew because he showed up in court and when I asked him he said point blank that he worked at the corporate office and was a consultant on the case---so much for honesty before the court by the guy in the silk suit.

By the way, use the ethics hotline. Use it often and use it wisely. They can't tell you what to do, but they can tell you what could or might happen and send you in the direction of some cases that might help you.

The law can be a scary thing. Come on everybody. Play fair. Fight nice. Do the right thing, Be like my friend, Bob Deems and fight for that three dollars a month for your client. Show the world what integrity and vigorous advocacy really is.

By the way when you are contemplating a lawsuit you are not allowed to say anything except that you will pursue all legal actions available to you. Do not mention anything else, or you may be reported for a violation of "Rule 5-100 Threatening Criminal, Administrative, or Disciplinary Charges." And yes, this also happened to me when the stooge filed the complaint against me in the previously mentioned case of the embezzler and the two child molesters. Because prior to moving forward on anything, I offered to

You Can't Do That!

help the embezzler and advised her that what she had done was a violation of certain penal statutes. In fact, I practically begged her to let me help her. And this was also used against me by the attorney who got the stooge to write a letter of complaint to the State Bar about me when the administrative issues were finished and a civil suit was foreseeable. Again, I had been told by another attorney that his clients would do anything to get rid of me, and they were making good their threats. This time, however, I feared for my life and even put a lock on my front gate. No one cared. Part of the reason the parents who sided with these two coaches were so upset with me was they were here in the United States illegally. In the end the child molester who was caught and pleaded guilty was deported by ICE. That is all I will say on that facet of the subject. Suffice it to say the child molester who was deported had been someone my own daughter looked up to and admired, had been to my home and to my child's birthday parties, and we considered him to be a family member. However when it came to the welfare of the children, none of that mattered; and I thought of Bob, and I did what I knew I had to do. I stood up for what was just, right and good; and I accomplished nothing----but what went around for that guy finally came around, He did time and was deported, but he is free and coaching water polo in Mexico, so who knows how many more innocents will be hurt at is hands, no thanks to the attorney who protected all of them in this, to USA swimming who gave them back their coaches cards, to the city who would not listen, and to everyone else who looked on and watched it all happen.

The bottom line here is be careful when it comes to whom you try to help; and even if you think you are helping a friend, don't, not without written precautions. Do not give unsolicited advice, even if you see they are breaking the law and you want with all your heart to help them. If someone files a complaint against you with the state bar, get an attorney. I did. I still have the right to practice law. I was not suspended.

When I tried to get an apology from the attorney who sat on the board he said he called the state bar and all they had done was decide not to take me to trial, and that did not mean I wasn't guilty. Again, here was another guy with the word jerk written across his forehead who conspired with the other side to get rid of me while he was supposed to be a non-partial quasi judicial trier of fact. Yes, I have had it all happen to me, and now I do my very best to keep my big mouth shut. I do not like living in fear, and there are very few people that I trust. I don't blame anyone who does not trust an attorney. Do you hear that, Bob? I sure miss you!

If you have any questions about the rules of ethics call the State Bar of California Ethics Hotline. Attorneys can call the Ethics Hotline from 9 a.m. until 5 p.m. (PST) on weekdays at 1-800-238-4427 (1-800-2-ETHICS) from within California or call 415-538-2150 from outside California. The hotline has been and is an

You Can't Do That!

invaluable resource to me and to other California attorneys. In any event, they can help you hold on to your sanity in what appears to be an insane world. By the way, you are under no obligation to report another attorney's violation of the Rules of Conduct.

Chapter Eleven
An Overview Of The Civility Toolbox

As you read the California Rules of Professional Conduct you will come to the conclusion they are way too short and that they leave many points you feel should be there, conspicuously absent. The Civility Toolbox entered the scene to point the way to wayward attorneys all across the State of California.

> "As officers of the court with responsibilities to the administration of justice, attorneys have an obligation to be professional with clients, other parties and counsel, the courts and the public. This obligation includes civility, professional integrity, personal dignity, candor, diligence, respect, courtesy, and cooperation, all of which are essential to the fair administration of justice and conflict resolution."
>
> **California Attorney Guidelines of Civility and Professionalism**

And there we have it, the words we love to read, the words by which all attorneys should properly conduct themselves. My favorite among these words, besides, integrity, is the word civility. I can't say every attorney I meet isn't civil, it is just that those who are not

You Can't Do That!

civil seem to outweigh in my mind, quite disproportionately, those who are. So now we have some words by which we can all abide. Did you know this was even out there? Let's take a look.

Exactly what are the California Attorney Guidelines of Civility and Professionalism? The California Attorney Guidelines of Civility and Professionalism are *voluntary goals* set in writing of the best practices of civility in the practice of law in the State of California. Hmmmm. My first question (before I even looked at what they said) was, "Will they work?" Then my next question was, "What do they say?" And why are there two versions of what attorneys are supposed to do and not do? The state bar says the two versions are complementary. One, with examples, illustrates the problem areas and best practices for each subject addresses. The two-page second version is a summary an attorney can carry when out of the office. (You know, in case the attorney forgets what good manners are.) The guidelines do not impose or dictate conduct, they have no bite, and no punishment can be enforced for failure to follow them. The Rules of Professional Conduct are the only rules that can be used to impose any sort of standard upon counsel by which counsel may receive reprimand, other than being found in contempt of court. Unlike the California Rules of Professional Conduct, the Supreme Court of California has not approved or mandated the guidelines, and they do not have the force of legislative enactments. So why even follow them? The bar says civility in the practice of law promotes effectiveness and enjoyment of the practice of law. (I would agree with that statement.) The bar adds they also promote economical client representation (and that I do not understand—perhaps it means if you are civil you spend less time fighting and there are fewer billable hours, and the client saves money; and that is the crux of the problem among attorneys—they like billable hours.) The bar tells is conduct that is not civil not only disserves clients, it demeans the profession and the American system of justice. So ask yourself, where do you think a guy who has to make a mortgage looks? I'll tell you. He looks to his pocket, and conflict pays; and that is the problem. And then by default that attorney is pursuing an interest adverse to his client—his own paycheck in the form of billable hours. I know I have argued and argued with various opposing counsel to resolve matters rather than litigate. They take my unwillingness to continue in it as a sign of weakness. Maybe it is. However, the State Bar of California says in the guidelines:

> "The Guidelines are intended to complement codes of professionalism adopted by bar associations in California. Individual attorneys are encouraged to make these guidelines their personal standards by taking the pledge that appears at the end. The Guidelines can be applicable to all lawyers regardless of practice area. Attorneys are encouraged to comply with both the spirit and letter of these guidelines, recognizing that complying with these guidelines does not in any way denigrate the attorney's duty of zealous representation."

CALIFORNIA ATTORNEY GUIDELINES OF CIVILITY AND PROFESSIONALISM
(Adopted July 20, 2007) **INTRODUCTION**

If the California State Bar says it, then it must be good, right? And the guidelines also tell us these were created out of or because of various local rules of court, which means someone is taking these things quite seriously. So, while they are only guidelines at the moment, it might behoove California counsel to pay attention to the latest version of 'Miss Manners' for California attorneys.

SECTION 1, RESPONSIBILITIES TO THE JUSTICE SYSTEM states:

"The dignity, decorum and courtesy that have traditionally characterized the courts and legal profession of civilized nations are not empty formalities. They are essential to an atmosphere that promotes justice and to an attorney's responsibility for the fair and impartial administration of justice."

The bar encourages us in this document to look to furthering justice and to offer out time to those people and organizations who cannot afford the costs of justice. And yes, this is what a good attorney should do. It is what I do. But you must still remember that those you represent can and may turn around and sue you for malpractice and/or report you to the California State Bar for any one of a number of breaches of the Rules of Professional Conduct. No one is perfect and we all make mistakes, but do not think when you volunteer to represent a person or an organization that because you are working for free they will not drive you, try to control you, and even turn on you. Trust no one. Do not use a volunteer representation as a training position. Make sure you are prepared and that you know your stuff. Take no chances.

You Can't Do That!

SECTION 6: SCHEDULING, CONTINUANCES AND EXTENSIONS OF TIME states:

"An attorney should consider the scheduling interests of the court, other counsel or party, and other participants, should schedule by agreement whenever possible, and should send formal notice after agreement is reached."

Now, I can tell you from personal experience that even though you follow this guideline, it may not be followed by your opposition. When I was in the hospital having my third child I was extremely ill with a severe case of eclampsia. As I lay there in a pre-convulsive state, shaking, I remembered I had responses to interrogatories due so I called my secretary to have her call my friend Bob to get an extension of time to answer. Bob returned the call and I lay there on the hospital bed as he said he could go into court and get the extension ordered with no problem, but the opposition (and this was the guy in the silk suit I mentioned earlier) would not agree to an extension of time to answer unless I answered every single question without objection. There I was all hooked up to various and sundry monitors going over the interrogatories in my mind, deciding if I could answer them without objection. Since I like being straightforward in my responses, I decided I could do it. Bob asked if I was sure, and I said, "Yes." The point of this is that a month earlier the wife of the silk suit was hospitalized for her pregnancy, and he asked me for an extension of time and I gave it to him. Bob pointed out this was a matter of professional courtesy, but the silk

You Can't Do That!

suit didn't care. I didn't regret granting him an extension, because I believe and believed in acting in a reasonable and professional manner; and maybe the guy in the silk suit just wanted Bob to take the matter to an emergency hearing so he could generate fees. All he looked like was a jerk. But then again, this was the same client that said they would no anything to get me off the case---a simple case to quiet title where they had a whole lot to hide, and they really did not want J.Q. Public to know they were hiding behind a law that flew in the face of common sense and allowed them to create an illusory contract. I haven't looked lately, but I imagine the law is still out there, protecting title insurance from their own negligence in searching a title. Someone should change that law, but I just don't have the strength anymore. I tried. Then right in the middle of everything I had this wonderful little baby, and I decided I needed to take care of myself and her, and so in the end, because my client wanted it, we settled. We were finally able to close title after five years of litigation, and that was all my client wanted in the first place. He also got a few other perks in the deal, like a fixed interest rate, etc.; but that is another matter altogether. I can only hope that what goes around really does come around. I am sure it will. I am never wrong about those things. Someone just needs to say, "You can't do that!" We need to stop the madness among us. Then we will be respected and revered, and they will stop making those jokes about the profession I love to hate; and I can go into the courtroom and simply enjoy the smell of the paper and the drama of it all.

CHAPTER TWELVE
Open The Box

So here we are with this box. What do we do with it? Maybe it's a Pandora's Box and we will release all manner of evil upon the world. It is more likely that what we will release is all good, so open the box. Let's bring civility into the world. Attorneys should read The Guidelines of Professionalism and Civility in all earnest. They cover just about everything we should be when it comes to being (as my mother used to put it) 'ladies and gentlemen.' Attorneys should serve a higher purpose, make the law right, serve the people, protect the underdog, and (yes) leap tall buildings with a single bound. They should not scare you to death when they serve papers. (By the way, my client, when he was served in that malicious prosecution case I spoke of earlier, was met at the door by the same process server with his hand in my client's morning newspaper. The process server was a really big guy and my client said he thought there was a gun in the rolled up newspaper and he nearly wet his pants.)

And so this is some of what 'Miss Manners' has in her box of tricks:

"An attorney should not serve papers to take advantage of an opponent's absence or to inconvenience the opponent, for instance by serving papers late on Friday afternoon or the day preceding a holiday."

"When serving papers, an attorney should allow sufficient time for opposing counsel to prepare for a court appearance or to respond to the papers."

"An attorney should not serve papers to take advantage of an opponent's absence or to inconvenience the opponent, for instance by serving papers late on Friday afternoon or the day preceding a holiday."

There doesn't appear to be anything about scaring someone half to death in the civility guidelines, but I do recall that shortly after that there was a case that said an attorney was responsible for the actions of his process server, and the courts have acted against attorneys who have violated notices of unavailability and do things like this, but why does it have to be done in the first place? These guys thought it was one big joke, and it is my opinion that attorneys will do just about anything if they think they can get away with it, and if they think it will gain them an advantage in a case. They know that (especially as to a plaintiff's attorney) the opposition can little afford prolonged litigation, and the stress on an opposition without a deep, deep pocket can be great. Missing work for unnecessarily

You Can't Do That!

lengthy depositions, taking time to answer interrogatories, produce a plethora of documents or to make motions to protect privacy and the like causes stress; and more than likely the settlement that comes after a couple of years of letters, meetings and discovery will be the opening amount the plaintiff's attorney asked for in the first place.

In my opinion, insurers' counsel and counsel for big business and the like are seriously out to destroy plaintiffs' counsel; and when that is done, no one will have any work at all. Therefore, what is really happening out there is no one is taking responsibility for anything they do. We are all like a bunch of children in a sandbox throwing sand at one another. Soon we will all be forbidden from playing in the sandbox.

There are many more suggestions in the box, and there probably should be more. All of these rules are based (primarily) on local rules of court from various jurisdictions throughout the state of California, which just goes to show us that the state of California has a serious ethics problem, that attorneys will probably do anything they can get away with doing when it comes to the opposition, and that just maybe their mothers didn't teach them anything---either that or there is a frat boy mentality out there that needs to stop. I have been given a filthy chair and had to ask for a clean one. I have watched multiple opposition attorneys group together, tell dirty jokes, whisper in my presence and laugh. I have had attorneys speak to judges in chambers by first name and have judges ask about

You Can't Do That!

family members who (for example) work for the FBI. I have been told not to interrupt when I am making an objection and I have seen other women have the same thing happen to them---I have even been told when making an objection to something a male client says to "let him finish," and been threatened with contempt when I ask ever so politely for a ruling on an objection---and more. I was told by one judge that I had a reputation for interrupting, which made me wonder why he was talking about me and with whom was he taking about me outside of the courtroom. (I pretty much knew, and when I went to that judge and asked that he recuse himself from hearing further cases with me, he said it was my problem and not his and I was polite, but I wanted to just scream. But do remember *this,* there are also rules for judicial conduct. Judges are also attorneys. I went back to the ethics hotline to ask what I could do. Basically, everything is a balancing act, and mostly it is just not worth it to risk the year to year relationship for the day to day result, because when a complaint is filed, the person against whom you filed the complaint knows it was you. They are told it was you.

And that again brings me back to the toolbox where they ask you not to seek sanctions unless absolutely necessary to show abuse. Let me tell you, I have asked for sanctions and attorneys fees every time I was forced to make a completely unnecessary motion to resolve a matter that over something that should have never happened in the first place---I have never had sanctions granted, never---and the word is that in the lower courts all you can really do is make a record for appeal. So there you are spending money you should not have to spend while the big guys on the other side tell jokes and laugh.

This is why we need the Civility Toolbox, but if you can't get sanctions for being forced to file a motion or to respond to a motion or to be served a frivolous lawsuit on your way to China, what can a few suggestions about how one should act actually accomplish? Those of us who do the right thing can only hope for the best, even if we want to tell all those attorneys who do that stuff anyway, because they can, that they should just be ashamed of themselves. And that is why I am writing this book. I am tired of screaming out, "You can't do that!" in my dreams.

The State Bar of California approved the Civility Guidelines on July 20, 2007, and shortly thereafter the various local bar associations, etc, followed and adopted it. Here is a list set forth in the civility guidelines:

• March 18, 2008, the Board of Directors of the Riverside County Bar Association approved and adopted the Guidelines.

• March 26, 2008, the Board of Directors of the Leo A. Deegan Inn of Court adopted a resolution approving and adopting the Guidelines.

• April 24, 2008, the San Diego County Bar Association introduced an updated Attorney Code of Conduct. The Attorney Code of conduct was a cornerstone of the bar association's 2008 Campaign on Civility, Integrity and Professionalism.

You Can't Do That!

• September 2008, a program on the Guidelines was given at the State Bar's annual meeting in Monterey, California. A similar program had been given at the annual meeting in 2007.

• June 11, 2008, the Joseph B. Campbell Inn of Court adopted the Guidelines.

• July 1, 2008, the Sacramento Superior Court recognized the existence of the Guidelines, effective this date. (Local rule 9.22)

• January 2009, the Schwartz/Levi American Inn of Court presented a program in civility in the practice of law.

• March 18, 2009, a program on the judge's role in ensuring civility and professionalism civility opened the 2009 Civil Law Institute sponsored by the California Center for Judicial Education and Research.

All in all, the guidelines are relatively new, so it remains to be seen if judges will act to enforce the parameters they pose, and more importantly if they will have a true effect on the state of the California State Bar Association and its members. Perhaps the ethics shown on television in the various shows about the law will have an effect and change the perceptions and the expectations of the public as well as all the attorneys out there. My mother always said there was no excuse for bad manners, and this is all this is---one big case of a bunch of people with some very bad manners, acting in a childlike fashion with no regard for what should be the acceptable bounds of society. In fact, I once had a client who characterized the actions of our opposition as amoral; and that is not a perception any of us want to have about any of us because it brings down, in general, the level of respect for attorneys everywhere.

Chapter Thirteen
Is That All There Is?

When I look at the Rules of Professional Conduct and the Guides of Civility, I can't help thinking, "Is that all there is?" You have to take an entire course on this stuff in law school and yet the amount to read, insofar as the actual rules and guidelines is so small; and when I went to law school there was only the rules. I only recently actually realized the Guidelines of Civility actually existed. I guess the law is about winning for most counsel. I would like to think the law is about leaving a mark on the world and about making a difference. My father was a musician, and he always stopped to help a person with a flat tire. At Thanksgiving, we always had a serviceman at our table. He would give you the shirt off of his back. My mother could make a silk purse out of a sow's ear. She always made the best of any situation. She told me stories about when she was a kid in the great depression and how the only movies they were allowed to see as kids were Shirley Temple movies. Perhaps that is our problem. We all have so much now that we have forgotten what it means to be polite and to feel. It can't be because both parents now work, because my mother *always* worked; and we were still raised with standards of civility.

Now it appears attorneys have to be told how to act and what is right. Remember when I said at the beginning of this book that a professor once told me that when you became an attorney your perception of what was right and wrong changed because it was based on the law? I really don't think that is the case. As attorneys we all need to take a step back and have a heart. In fact, I just donated my fees and costs to a case where a child was getting a multi-organ transplant and was involved in a products liability injury. The insurer waived its rights in subrogation. Why? They said I had a heart and they also had a heart. Perhaps it is true that one good deed *can* beget another.

The guidelines of civility clearly say attorneys should remember their primary goals are to negotiate in a manner that accurately represents their client and the purpose for which they were retained, and that they should successfully and (in a timely manner) conclude issues in a way that accurately represents the parties' intentions, with the *least likely* potential for litigation. They do not say we should be as uncooperative as possible in order to present more billable hours to our clients or that we should make it our goal to do anything to "get rid of" opposing counsel, or to threaten, harass or make opposing counsel not only feel ill and require medical attention, but also make them fear for their lives. And yes, to the attorneys who have done that to me (and I assume others) your mothers would be ashamed of you if they knew what you are doing and what you did.

One of my law professors (I had a lot of great law professors) stood in front of the class on the first day of law school and announced that if any of us ever got tired of practicing law, or discouraged by the practice of law, there were other things we could do. He pointed out that he left his New York practice to teach law school and to write pornography after doing a stint as a hippie---I am not sure in what order all of that happened, but it stuck with me. Being able to practice law is useful, even if you decide to fill vending machines. There is life after law, even if once a lawyer, always a lawyer. As for me? I started my own publishing company and have as of this date 209 titles and fourteen writers! And yes, I am still practicing law with the occasional case that always drives me crazy. People beg me to represent them. I do still love the smell of the paper and the feel of the courtroom. In fact, I was in court today and have another hearing shortly. I am now simply practicing law in a different way most of the time. I practice law in the transactional sense. But I have done it all, and everything has been done to me.

You Can't Do That!

When I venture into the courtroom, Bob is always there with me---I Blame my inability to not help the underdog on him. It's that old integrity thing. It helps to be a lawyer when you are running your own publishing company. And we do not self-publish. We are a traditional publishing house. I just have the advantage of always being able to get *my* books published. And when someone steals a trademark (and I do have a couple of them) I yell, "You can't do that!" The attorneys still do whatever they want, and you have to decide whether litigation is cost effective, but at least you have the tools!

Chapter Fourteen
Is That Really The Case?

Various cases affirm and define the California Rules of Professional Conduct. For example, the case *Segal v. State Bar* 44 Cal.3d 1077, 245 Cal. Rptr. 404 (1988) stands for the premise that an attorney *must* decline representation where the attorney lacks the time and the resources to pursue the client's case with reasonable diligence. In *Cosenza v. Kramer* 152 Cal.App.3d 1100, 200 Cal.Rptr. 18 (1984) the court held that an attorney has the responsibility *not* to pursue a client's frivolous appeal just because a client demands it. Also, a delay is deemed frivolous if the motive of the request for a delay is to outlive the other party through appeals. *Hendricks v. Pappas*, 82 Cal.App.2d 774, 187 P.2d 436 (1947). An attorney must maintain only legal or just actions. *Canatella v.*

You Can't Do That!

California (9th Cir.) 304 F.3d 843 (2002), *Sorensen v. State Bar,* 52 Cal.3d 1036 (1991).

You can also get all the ethics opinions from 1965 until the present, by simply going to the State Bar of California website at http://ethics.calbar.ca.gov/Ethics/Opinions/2009176toPresent.aspx

The truth is a lot of good attorneys at one time or another suffer burnout and take a break from the practice of law. I have heard lawyers say they are just tired of looking over their shoulders all the time. The practice of law can also be a dangerous thing, because people in all sorts of areas of the law seem to get very worked up about their cases, and perhaps their expectations are simply too high. This is why you must begin your contractual obligations with them by stressing there are no guarantees as to the outcome of a case, and should probably include that disclaimer in your attorney fee agreement with them. At best any outcome is a fifty-fifty proposition, and in the state of California filing fees alone can be more than your client can afford. In fact, I couldn't afford myself, so it is a good thing I have my own attorney, me. And at least I won't report myself to the state bar, so I am a perfect client, even though it is said the attorney who represents himself has a fool for a client. In any event I only represent myself in the transactional arena. I am really not litigious when it comes to me, as strange as that may seem.

You Can't Do That!

And that reminds me, be aware of the overly litigious client as well. They may mean trouble for you. And if you do not get along with a client, do recommend they seek another counsel before you get too far into the litigation because this may save you a lot of grief later.

I think the best thing you can do for both yourself and your client is to do the best *by* your client. A client can't ask for more. Beware, be aware and be careful, because it is not a nice world out there.

Again, if you have an ethics question you can call the state bar hotline at 1-800-238-4427 (1-800-2-ETHICS) within California, or you can call 415-538-2150 from outside of California. If there is another attorney you trust, ask his opinion, and/or go to the State Bar of California website for the California State Bar ethics opinions at http://ethics.calbar.ca.gov/Ethics/Opinions/2009176toPresent.aspx.

If you like, you can also purchase a copy of the Rules of Professional Conduct and The State Bar Act (Publication 250) 2006, for $20 by mail, and $15 if picked up in person from either the Los Angeles or San Francisco offices of the California State Bar Association. Pre-payment is required. Send your payment by mail to:

The State Bar of California
Professional Competence
180 Howard Street
San Francisco, CA 94105.

You Can't Do That!

At the end of the day you may still be shouting, "You can't do that!" but having all the information at hand may at least give you a measure of comfort.

Chapter Fifteen

In The News

Involuntary inactive enrollment was ordered by the California State Bar in July of 2010 for three Southern California attorneys: Eric Douglas Johnson of Los Angeles, Mark Alan Shoemaker of Long Beach and Brian Colombana of Lake Forest. I say bravo for the California State Bar Association!

Besides these three involuntary inactive enrollments, the bar's Office of Chief Trial Counsel (as of July 2010) also obtained the resignations of 13 attorneys involved in foreclosure misconduct since the creation of the Loan Modification Task Force in April 2009. Five loan modification trials were pending as of July 2010 and another 2,000 investigations were underway. The details and the reasoning behind the above mentioned judgments can be found at the

You Can't Do That!

California Bar Journal website. For details of the above cases see: http://www.calbarjournal.com/July2010/TopHeadlines/TH3.aspx

In San Francisco on Sept. 23, 2010 the State Bar's Office of Chief Trial Counsel also obtained an agreement from Orange County lawyer Mark Alan Shoemaker to be disbarred.

Shoemaker, from Santa Ana, was the sixth lawyer to agree to disbarment because of complaints from 18 homeowners who got little or nothing for their money when seeking help changing the terms of mortgage agreements and avoiding foreclosure. Details can be found at: http://www.calbar.ca.gov/AboutUs/News/201027.aspx

The State Bar found Shoemaker "failed to perform legal services competently, failed to refund unearned fees, inadequately communicated with clients, failed to account for advanced fees and costs, charged an unconscionable fee, failed to deposit funds in a Client Trust Account and aided a non-attorney in the practice of law," and Shoemaker also agreed that his misconduct demonstrated "a pattern of willfully failing to perform services and a habitual disregard for his clients."

However, these are just *a few* of the people who have been swindled and cheated by attorneys who somehow feel it is okay to take (for example) a disproportionate amount in fees from their clients, often in the form of taking a trust deed interest in real property, foreclosing on that property, and recovering in fees either property value or actual dollars upon sale of that property worth more than what should have been tendered for reasonable attorneys fees. People and property have always been good targets. I have advised individuals to whom this has happened to file complaints with the state bar. I have informed the court of conflicts of interest when an attorney obtains a pecuniary interest in property in litigation that exceeds reasonable attorneys fees. I have seen it all and heard the justifications. I do not agree with them. It must take a plethora of individuals all appearing all at once across the country to get things moving. When it comes to real property and the fleecing of the ordinary person, the ordinary everyday person is an easy mark. And so the guys in the silk suits continue to prosper and laugh as they wash junior lien holders in fraudulent conveyance schemes and as little old ladies lose life savings and are forced into the streets. I do believe things are that bad, and I do know there is a lot of money to be made and lost by assigning assets to attorneys to pay fees. I had one client who lost seven million dollars and a block of downtown property in one year, and the law firm who did this showed up at a business bankruptcy hearing representing a creditor. I discovered the conflict and filed a motion with the court to have that counsel removed, and a new law firm appeared on the scene shortly thereafter. The next time I went to court I was asked who I was going to tar and feather that day.

All I can say is you must be diligent and protect your client. The court did not report that law firm to the California State Bar, but my client did, and the only response he got (even as he submitted two inches of paper evidence) was they needed more evidence to proceed. I was hoping the law firm would have to disgorge it ill gotten proceeds as the statute of limitations had passed on them. My client had no such luck, although I am not sure if he sent a reply to the state bar. Somehow that was okay, and what is happening now isn't? I failed to see the difference, and I absolutely in my heart believe this does not comport nor comply with the rules, taking an interest in real property that is part of a pending litigation, or that is in litigation, to secure a fee is not proper, especially if the interest unreasonably exceeds the value of legal services rendered. Few agree with me, especially if this is what they do. I guess if you can get away with it, then you do it. I mean they do it. I would never do it or recommend it. I like being able to live with myself. But then that is why people want to get rid of me. I am a challenge to their modus operandi. Most of the time people do not know what is happening to them, much less that it is wrong. Individuals look to an attorney for counsel and help in a time of dire need. Attorneys hold the highest responsibility to their clients. When attorneys breach the oaths they made with the state bar and the courts in this fashion, it makes me again want to scream, "You can't do that!"

Someone must stop the madness. Let it stop with you and me.

CHAPTER SIXTEEN
Everyone Else Is Doing It!

When I used to say, "Everyone else is doing it, so why can't I?" my mother used to ask me, "If everyone was jumping off a bridge, would you jump off a bridge, too?" Another favorite phrase of hers was, "Do as I say and not as I do."

Now it is quite true that attorneys are not the only ones being plagued with ethics violations and scandals. And while you may want to say, "Do as I say and not as I do," attorneys are officers of the court, sworn to uphold the letter of the law, to coin a popular phrase from not so recent politics, even if we are not alone in this ethics quagmire.

1. On July 22, 2010 the news reported A House investigative committee had charged New York Rep. Charles Rangel with

multiple ethics violations, dealing a serious blow to the former Ways and Means chairman and complicating Democrats' election-year outlook.

2. On July 30, 2010 the newspapers reported the House panel had accused New York Rep. Charles B. Rangel of 13 ethics violations, placing his storied 40-year political career in jeopardy and *guaranteeing* Democrats an election-year headache.

3. On August 13, 2010 the news reported that a grand jury had indicted Democratic Senate candidate Alvin Greene Friday, for showing pornography to a student at the University of South Carolina.

4. In August 2010, Maxine Waters, a democrat from California, was accused by her colleagues in congress of using her position to secure bailout money for a bank in which her husband held an interest. The bank received $12 million in bailout funds.

5. In Kansas on October 30, 2010 it was reported that Candidate for Secretary of State Kris Kobach (R) faced criticism from a press conference where Kobach raised issues of voter fraud, and the Kansas Democratic Party announced they would file charges against Kobach for ethical violations over campaign donations.

You Can't Do That!

6. In March 2010 it was reported that in Kentucky two longtime employees of Louisville-Jefferson County Metro Government resigned after an audit revealed that the former employees violated the city's purchasing and personnel rules. Melissa Mershon, former director of the Neighborhoods Department, and Carol Butler, a special assistant in the department, submitted their resignations

7. On October 30, 2010, it was reported that the Florida State Ethics Commission had found probable cause of financial disclosure violations by their incoming Senate President Mike Haridopolos. The Merritt Island Republican is accused of failing to fully disclose his financial interests from 2004 through 2008.

8. On October 28, 2010 it was reported that Barbara Boxer would face ethics complaints because she asked teachers to send students to work for her campaign. The Howard Jarvis Taxpayers Association notified the Los Angeles Unified School District and the Los Angeles Board of Education that, in "abject ignorance of California state law," the political campaign of Senator Barbara Boxer openly solicited teachers to urge their students to volunteer and work for her campaign.

9. n December 2009 it was reported that US Rep. Nathan Deal, who ran for Governor of Georgia in the Republican primary,

was under investigation over potential ethics violations exposed by the *Atlanta Journal-Constitution.* According to records obtained by the AJC through the state's Open Records Act, both the Office of Congressional Ethics and the U.S. House Committee on Standards of Official Conduct had inquired about Deal's role in a 20-year business arrangement with the state that earned his company $1.5 million from 2004 through 2008.

10. On March 4, 2010 it was reported that Honolulu, Hawaii Councilmember Rod Tam was being forced to pay back $11,700 in city funds he spent on meals the city Ethics Commission said were not legitimate city business. He was also fined $2,000 for the ethics violation and misuse of city funds.

11. On October 30, 2010 the Chicago tribune reported that a former top aide to Cook County Board President Todd Stroger, who faces criminal charges in a contracting scandal, also violated four ethics provisions. Carla Oglesby, Stroger's one-time deputy chief of staff, broke conflict-of-interest rules and a prohibition on county employees benefiting from contracts. She resigned.

Of course I could go on and on with these various violations and breach of ethics from all corners of our society,

You Can't Do That!

and I suppose we could all blame it on the other guy, and say that because they were doing it, it was okay for us to do it. I think most of these breaches are based on two things, no maybe three. Those three things are a lust for power, greed, and weakness of the human spirit. When Bill Clinton was asked why he made his indiscretions, he said it was because he could. Nixon clearly thought he could get away with Watergate. So why do people lie and cheat and break the rules? It is probably because they can. And they will use all means available to them whether ethical or not if they can get what they want and if they can get rid of you. Fear for yourself and toe the line. Toeing the line of ethics sometimes takes great courage. It always involves morality and great integrity. Be good because you want to be good, not because you fear you will get caught. And remember that the truth is an easy thing to remember, because it is, after all the truth, the whole truth and nothing but the truth, so help me God.

CHAPTER SEVENTEEN
Anything Goes

Cole porter wrote the song, and Ella Fitzgerald sang it, but the lyrics seem more applicable today than ever.

Times have changed,
And we've often rewound the clock,
Since the Puritans got a shock,
When they landed on Plymouth Rock,
If today, any shock they should try to stand,
Steads' landing on Plymouth Rock,
Plymouth Rock would land on them.

In olden days a glimpse of stockings,
Was looked on as something shocking,
Now heaven knows,
Anything goes.

Good authors too who once knew better words,
Now only use four-letter words,
Writing prose,
Anything Goes.

You Can't Do That!

> The world has gone mad today,
> And good's bad today,
> And black's white today,
> And days night today,
> When most guys today,
> That women prize today,
> Are just silly gigolos.
>
> So though I'm not a great romance,
> I know that I'm bound to answer,
> When you propose,
> Anything goes.

Is it really true that today anything goes? Is the Civility Toolbox our gift to open so we can usher in a new respect for attorneys across the Golden State of California? When you hear that Cole Porter song do you want to break into a tap dance? Or is it all of the above, or none of the above? Is our judicial system poised to disintegrate beneath one big pile of dirty tricks? Have attorneys, like politicians all reverted to mud-slinging and to doing anything they have to do to get rid of the other guy and to win? Perhaps all of this is being done because legal cases and election campaigns really can't be won on their merits. At what price are we wearing the façade of success?

The truth is "Anything Goes" was written by Cole Porter for his musical *Anything Goes* in 1934. Many of the original lyrics featured humorous and dated references to various figures of scandal and gossip in Depression Era high society. And the song was controversial and written to point out all the things society was doing wrong. It was very political and meant to stir hearts toward a more puritan society.

Ironically, it would appear that the better the times, the worse morality among us seems to get. How much money do we really need to live? If we talk about sharing our wealth with others, even our own wealth, we are labeled communists. Meanwhile, insurance companies and big businesses rule the world, and we are manipulated with the help of attorneys by dot com economies and economies built on fraudulent real estate deals, blaming victims for not staying away from deals they knew or should have known they could not afford, but were talked into them by bankers and attorneys. How can you blame them? They only wanted what they thought everyone else had, so they took a hand and jumped off the bridge into the water, eventually out to the homeless on the street.

Rights to file and old fashioned bankruptcy and to start anew are now only afforded businesses thanks to our legislature. People must pay back what they owe, except in very, very narrow circumstances. Everyone is looking to protect what little they have and attorneys have a whole new business, debt reorganization---but even in that there are breaches of ethics.

Government employees in the state of California are awarding themselves exorbitant pension packages as the education system falls further and further into disrepair. Everyone talks about entitlements as if taxpayers haven't been paying into these funds for years, and as if government hasn't been dipping into these accounts to pay for other things. There is a reason unemployment benefits come from something called "unemployment insurance," and that is because it comes from insurance for which you have had to pay for years. In fact, if you haven't worked and paid into it, you simply do not get to collect from it.

No one should receive more than they deserve, but since you earned it, you should get it. And it is also true that everyone should pay their fair share.

All of these things are intertwined in our ethics and our attitude towards ethics. Our state of being in regard to legal ethics is merely a reflection of what is going on in the outside world. The trouble is---the outside world is going to hell in a hand basket, and we as attorneys, officers of the court and upholders of the law are supposed to be above it all. It is of great concern to me as an attorney that we are not above it all, and it makes me want to scream out over and over again, "You can't do that!"

CHAPTER EIGHTEEN
So Much To Know, So Little Time

If you look on the California State Bar website you can find all the code sections that are related to attorney ethics throughout the titles of each of the California Code chapters, by section number. http://rules.calbar.ca.gov/SelectedLegalAuthority/RelatedStatutes.aspx

It is really way too much to put in here, but I mention it because it is worth knowing it is there. This definitely falls into the so much to know so little time category for me.

The Constitution of California Relevant Provisions (in the Constitution of the State of California) as they pertain to the California State Bar are found in Article VI, sections 6, 8 and 9 and are linked through the California State Bar Website as follows:

You Can't Do That!

http://rules.calbar.ca.gov/SelectedLegalAuthority/ConstitutionExcerpts.aspx

At the following address you can also find a link that will take you to the California Rules of Court, but you need to also know the local rules of each of the courts in the State of California in which you practice. The San Diego County courts have further implemented rules at times for various courtrooms, which means even more to know.

http://rules.calbar.ca.gov/SelectedLegalAuthority/CaliforniaRulesofCourt.aspx

I know this is true because I once went to a hearing, and the judge asked me if I had requested in advance for permission to speak under his own court rule. At that time judges were even moving from court to court, and so I am now in the habit of calling the clerk as soon as a case is assigned to a judge to find out if there are any special rules of which I should be aware (a nearly impossible task otherwise).

And then we have the State Bar Act, also linked to the Rules of Professional conduct, and you can go to the links for that at:

http://rules.calbar.ca.gov/SelectedLegalAuthority/TheStateBarAct.aspx

If the truth is to be told, I don't know what we did before we had the internet. Perhaps we all behaved better than we do now. I do know that Bob told me there was a time when all you did was

You Can't Do That!

take your client straight to trial. There were no discovery rules, motions, etc. You discovered what you needed to discover at trial and that was that. Supposedly, all of this stuff began so we could be encouraged to settle matters and not even go to trial, and the Rules of Civility encourage that---but it seems to me that the box we opened with this was a Pandora's Box that has allowed as the final result, litigation to run amok with breaches of duty and misdeeds of unprofessional conduct, which all makes me again want to scream, "You can't do that!"

You Can't Do That!

CHAPTER NINETEEN
What's Next?

The Selected Legal Authority relating to the Practice of Law and The State Bar of California as set forth by The State Bar of California is as follows:

- Constitution of California (Relevant Provisions)
- The State Bar Act (Business & Professions Code §§ 6000 et seq.)
- California Rules of Court, Rule of Court 9.7 Online reporting by attorneys. (*Effective February 1, 2010)*
- Related Statutes Regarding Professional Conduct, Discipline of Attorneys and Duties of the State Bar of California

http://rules.calbar.ca.gov/SelectedLegalAuthority.aspx

California Rule of Court 9.7 states in pertinent part: "To maintain the roll of attorneys required by rule 9.6 and to facilitate communications by the State Bar with its members, each member must use an online membership account on a secure system provided by the State Bar to report a current:

(1) Office address and telephone number, or if none, another address; and

(2) An e-mail address not to be disclosed on the State Bar's Web site or otherwise to the public without the member's consent."

Optionally it also includes the following:

"A member may also use an online membership account to:

(1) Provide an e-mail address for disclosure to the public on the State Bar Web site; and

(2) Provide additional information as authorized by statute, rule or Supreme Court directive, or as requested by the State Bar."

The bottom line is they have to know where to find us and how to get in touch with us for whatever purpose they desire. To me, with my personal experience, that can actually be a frightening proposition. Not only is our profession not respected, those in the profession are basically harassing one another and breaking all the rules and so are the clients. Well, perhaps not everyone breaks the rules, but having it happen even once to you, even a part of what has happened to me, can be extremely frightening and can cause you to lock your house and gate where you live in the country and buy a big dog. In fact during the title insurance/bank fraudulent conveyance case, my beautiful German shepherd also disappeared while I was in China, and my good childhood friend who had been a court reporter for twenty-five years at the time, told me. "First they take your dog, and then they rob you. They will do anything, trust me. I know and I have seen it all." Since she had been a court reporter longer than I had practiced law I listened when she told me to be careful. And when another attorney who was like me drove off the road in the middle of the night, I did wonder if someone drove him off that road to his death. Practicing law is a dangerous proposition. You can stick with safe cases, if you can find them; but when a guy comes in and fires a gun in the courtroom in a divorce case, you tremble. (At least *that* didn't happen to me.)

And if a complaint is filed against you with the California State Bar Association, get a lawyer right away, even if the complaint is a frivolous one. This is one area where an attorney who represents himself, truly has a fool for a client. I happened to call Attorney Art Margolis after my initial response. I found him on a CEB state bar on line ethics course. He was great. Within two weeks it was finished, and I am still practicing law. Even when you do the right thing, the opposition can twist it in all directions. And as I said earlier, it was the group with the embezzler and the two child molesters, protected

You Can't Do That!

by shield of counsel who did this to me because as opposition counsel had threatened, his clients would do anything to get rid of me. The counsel prepared the complaint against me and had the stooge sign it. How do I know this? Only an attorney would know the legalese put in that complaint against me. It was another dirty trick, was itself against the Rules of Professional Conduct as as a material misrepresentation before the State Bar, and was outrageous and not provable against counsel or his law firm because the stooge filed the papers. It was no less than reprehensible. I screamed as loudly as I could, "You can't do that!" but without my attorney, Art Margolis, no one heard my voice. The moral of this story is that if you are reported to the state bar, get an attorney immediately and save yourself a lot of grief. You can do no good if you are stripped of your right to practice law, and that is exactly what the bad guys out there want to do. They want to stop you from practicing law, so that you will not expose their wrongs. But, as I have found, it may take awhile, but eventually all the roosters come home to roost. I may be a simple country attorney, but at least I have high moral standards, and I can most certainly live with myself. I even sent my attorney flowers.

You Can't Do That!

CHAPTER TWENTY
Don't Count On Anyone To Stop It

I went to court for a Settlement Conference hearing on a fairly simple personal injury case. I don't really remember that case, but what I do remember is the oppositions' counsels (and there were two of them) submitted ex-parte a joint *confidential* brief which they did not serve on me. I remember being incensed that I had no opportunity to respond to this *confidential* brief, and I expressed my upset to the judge. (This was the same judge that had told me a few years earlier that I was interrupting—but he had forgotten all about it—or he had reached a different opinion about me. In any event we were getting along.) He took us each into chambers. They went first. When I got into chambers he told me not to worry. The brief was so bad he didn't even understand what they were saying, and he added, "But I can understand every single word of what you say.

You Can't Do That!

You are really a good writer." I was still upset they were allowed to submit a *confidential* brief, but he encouraged me and them to just settle the matter. Before we left, we had settled the case, and the settlement was sufficient in amount to make me happy and to make my client happy, so I let it all go. However, to this day it still bothers me that these two bozos were allowed to submit a confidential brief, which in essence was an ex parte communication with the judge. They were not reported to the California State Bar, and they got away with breaking the rules of professional conduct just like the attorney for the embezzler and the two child molesters did. Since these matters directly involved the court, you would think the court on its own motion would call for sanctions, but it didn't happen. That's where I learned I could not ever absolutely count on the court to help me or even to enforce the Rules of Professional Conduct. I suppose the worst of the worst eventually get slapped on the wrist or something, but I really do not know. In the case of when I was reported to the state bar I was told the State bar was really mad at those guys, but the state bar never did anything about it. How could they? They used a stooge---all of them---from the local swim association right up the ladder to USA Swimming. And as I said, I know for a fact, from my own complaints about child molestation given to USA Swimming, that they never promptly (or even ever in my case) investigated our allegations of sexual abuse. Recent statements made to the contrary by USA Swimming that they

You Can't Do That!

promptly investigate all allegations of sexual abuse are without merit. (And by the way, my good friend Bob told me to use the words 'without merit' rather than accuse the opponent or anyone of being the liars they more than likely really are.)

I guess the point I am making is---those entities, the court and the state bar have the inherent authority to act on their own motions. Therefore, if the court or the state bar observes first hand an injustice, do they not have the duty to do something about it? In my case, apparently not. The sad thing is that once those things get done, they cannot only not be undone, they additionally serve as bragging fodder for other legal lunkheads who think they can get away with doing the same thing. When that happens justice is not served. The image of the legal system is not served. The innocent are harmed. Is not the legal system supposed to protect the innocent from all harm. Are we not all held to the highest of standards? Apparently this is not the case, and this is why I say to count on no one but yourself. Then, at least, you will not be disappointed. And if you are disappointed, you will only be disappointed with yourself.

Oh, and I almost forgot. Just yesterday I went to court for a court ordered case management conference and opposition counsel didn't even bother to show. Once again I was amazed, If it was I, I feel certain I would have been sanctioned. We have settled the case, and I told the court that; but I have been waiting for over a month for the settlement papers. Maybe the court sent the guy a notice of

You Can't Do That!

sanctions for failure to appear. I don't know. But if you miss a traffic hearing on a ticket you get, you get charged a large fine for failure to appear on top of the ticket. How could the guy just ignore an order sent by the court? AND I reminded him with three or so phone calls and daily email, and when I finally got a response from him he said he was in the mountains on a vacation! He is a partner in a 100 attorney law firm and he couldn't have someone appear for him? You can't do that! However, he did; and I have been worried ever since, greatly worried about the state of our settlement agreement. I happen to be a good guy. I think I saved his butt.

The good thing about being both a writer and owning a publishing company is that I can always have the very last word. And so I will continue to scream as loudly as I can, "You can't do that!"

Chapter Twenty-One
Two Wrongs Never Make a Right

Just because there are a dozen guys against you, or even two of them from two different defendants and they seem to agree, that doesn't mean that you are automatically wrong, because two or more wrongs never make a right, just ask my mother.

The thing is that when you are up against multiple defendants as plaintiff's counsel, it seems you become the common enemy. Therefore there is a feeding frenzy by the sharks, and they go after you.

This also gives them the courage to do what they would or may not otherwise do, and that is to throw their ethics out the window and go on an attack to gain a common advantage. This is sometimes referred to as my enemy's enemy is my friend. That is, even if the parties should be at each other's throats to place blame, you are the common enemy.

This is a clever move, and you wish one of them would side with you, but it is unlikely to happen. The end result is the unethical attack receives support and there is an all out feeding frenzy.

Now the rules of civility that are in the "Civility Toolbox" tell us we are supposed to not ask for sanctions for just anything, which is why you may hope the court will step in and act for you. However, as I pointed out earlier, this scenario is unlikely and you will be on your own.

You will not be able to convince these boys that they are hurting the legal profession by breaking the law in their attempt to rid themselves of you. They are caught up in a legal morass fueled by the money of their often deep pocketed clients, and if one of the pockets isn't so deep, it will still side with the deep pocket defendant in the hope they will pick up the cost of ridding themselves of you.

It happens. It's life. Fight with all your might. Hold out as long as you can against the tide of evil, and either go to trial or settle. Sometimes might does make right and that is a fact of life. When that low ball written offer comes along you are ethically required to present the offer to your client, and if your client accepts then that is that. Disappointment in the outcome will be mixed with relief because you may never have to see these jerks again. Luckily there are thousands of attorneys in the State of California.

You Can't Do That!

That brings us to why attorneys act like jerks. As I have stated before, attorneys used to practice from year to year, month to month and day to day, knowing they would meet counsel again in the court system. Now there are so many of us, we may never meet again after an initial case. Because of this, some of us will do anything, even break the rules, and if they can side together against a common denominator that might be you, they will. It doesn't seem so bad to them when two or more attorneys break rules together, and so they do it. It's the gang mentality, and they play the role of the bully. It makes them feel very important and full of self worth.

And you will want to scream oh so very loudly, "You can't do that!" Perhaps someone will hear.

Chapter Twenty-Two
State Bar Opinion #1981-62

The state bar has issued many ethics opinions. This chapter and those following will discuss a few of these opinions.

The first opinion we will look at is based on the following question, something I have discussed earlier in this book: May an attorney ethically take promissory notes or liens as security for fees? It is formal opinion no. 1981-62. The short answer is as follows: "An attorney may take a promissory note or obtain a security interest to protect the attorney's fees for services, subject to compliance with rule 5-101 of the Rules of Professional Conduct of the State Bar." So what is rule 5-101 of the state bar? Rule 5-101 of the State Bar states: "A member of the State Bar shall not enter into a business transaction with a client or knowingly acquire an ownership, possessory, security or other pecuniary interest adverse to a client

You Can't Do That!

unless (1) the transaction and terms in which the member of the State Bar acquires the interest are fair and reasonable to the client and are fully disclosed and transmitted in writing to the client in manner and terms which should have reasonably been understood by the client, (2) the client is given a reasonable opportunity to seek the advice of independent counsel of the client's choice on the transaction, and (3) the client consents in writing thereto."

It used to be that historically an attorney could not acquire an interest in property or a lien because it represented an interest adverse to the client. It is now held in this opinion that it is unethical to require or obtain a lien interest against the property of the client if the provisions of rule 5-101 are not followed. In evaluating whether a lien interest should be taken against a client, you are probably on a slippery slope. First the client has to fully understand the scope of what he or she is doing, and he or she also has to have adequate opportunity to seek the advice if independent counsel. However, even more important than that is the proposition that the lien must represent a fair and reasonable fee. In the case I discussed earlier, an attorney took property free and clear worth several million dollars, when the services rendered were clearly not worth the value of the property taken in lien. Also, at the onset the attorney knew or should have known based on the circumstances of the case, that it would be impossible for the client to pay attorneys fees after a certain point. In fact, the client was at that point and that is why he was asked to

You Can't Do That!

sign over a lien interest in his real property. The property consisted of both residential and commercial property and more than one lien. I believe the attorney alleged $300,00.00 (three hundred thousand dollars) of owed fees. He took over five million in property as payment. When I came to represent the client in a business bankruptcy proceeding. The firm I challenged with the conflict of interest issue was the same firm that took the lien on the property. I didn't find out the extent of this until later in the litigation when I asked to look at old legal papers from another proceeding.

I have told attorneys I believe this process is flawed, dangerous and wrong, and yes, I do shout, "You can't do that!" but no one really listens.

The State Bar came to this opinion by reviewing the history of the law and decisions and an opinion by the ABA. The opinion is advisory only and is not intended to modify existing law. My personal opinion is you should never do this. And if you do foreclose on a property you should take from the proceeds only that which is owed to you, adhering to the fair market value rule, meaning you should not undercut the value of the property to sell to a relative or friend just to make sure it comes within the reasonable fee rule. And if you have a lien interest, and gain more in dollars than you are owed, the difference in value should be properly returned to the client. If you sit on the lien and allow the client to keep his or her interest in the amount owed until the client can take a loan out on the property to repay you or sell the property to pay your reasonable fees, then there should be no problem. However, this is not what I see happening out there in real life and this is why I am appalled and continue to shout, "You can't do that!"

However, this is the opinion of one attorney only, is not meant to give specific advice on the law. For specific advice on any area of the law, please consult your own attorney. Laws are living and changing things. So are the Rules of Professional Conduct. Beware and be aware.

Part of the proposed amendment to the rules referencing this matter reads as follows:

"Rule 1.8.1 Business Transactions with a Client and Acquiring Interests Adverse to the Client

A lawyer shall not enter into a business transaction with a client; or knowingly acquire an ownership, possessory, security, or other pecuniary interest adverse to a client, unless each of the following requirements has been satisfied:

(a) The transaction or acquisition and its terms are fair and reasonable to the client and are fully disclosed and transmitted in writing to the client in a manner that reasonably can be understood by the client; and (b) The client either is represented in the transaction or acquisition by an independent lawyer of the client's choice or is advised in writing by the lawyer to seek the advice of an independent lawyer of the client's choice and is given a reasonable opportunity to
seek that advice; and . . .[(b) omitted by author]

You Can't Do That!

(c) The client thereafter consents in writing to the terms of the transaction or the terms of the acquisition and the lawyer's role in the transaction or acquisition, including whether the lawyer is representing the client in the transaction or acquisition."

PROPOSED RULES OF PROFESSIONAL CONDUCT
(Adopted by the Board of Governors on July 24, 2010 and September 22, 2010. Rules of Professional Conduct must be approved by the Supreme Court of California in order to become operative.

You Can't Do That!

CHAPTER TWENTY-THREE
State Bar Opinion #2009-178

The following is an ethics opinion regarding attorney's fees and settlement where the attorney wants to include a Civil Code Section 1542 waiver in the agreement with his client. The issues are: "Is it ethically proper for an attorney who is settling a fee dispute with a client to include a general release and a Civil Code section 1542 waiver in the settlement agreement? Does the existence of a legal malpractice claim against the attorney alter the ethical propriety of including a general release and section 1542 waiver in the settlement agreement?"

The opinion states an attorney must inform the client of any malpractice claim the client may have against the attorney. And if the attorney is considering entering into a settlement agreement with the client that would limit his or her malpractice, the attorney must

You Can't Do That!

advise the client of his or her right to seek independent counsel regarding the settlement agreement and should also consider withdrawing from the case.

The opinion further states with particularity that the attorney should:

"1. Comply with rule 3-400(B) by advising the client of the right to seek independent counsel regarding the settlement and giving the client an opportunity to do so;

2. Advise the client that the lawyer is not representing or advising the client as to the settlement of the fee dispute or the legal malpractice claim; and

3. Fully disclose to the client the terms of the settlement agreement, in writing, including the possible effect of the provisions limiting the lawyer's liability to the client, unless the client is represented by independent counsel."

http://ethics.calbar.ca.gov/LinkClick.aspx?fileticket=xW7YfO4JIg8%3d&tabid=837

The state bar relies on the following authority in this opinion:

1. 2-100, 3-300, 3-310, 3-400, and 3-500 of the Rules of Professional Conduct of the State Bar of California.

2. Business and Professions Code section 6068, subdivision (m).

You Can't Do That!

Civil Code section 1542

Section 1542 provides that: "A general release does not extend to claims which the creditor does not know or suspect to exist in his or her favor at the time of executing the release, which if known by him or her must have materially affected his or her settlement with the debtor."

The truth is everyone commits malpractice at some time or another, whether or not counsel even realizes it. In my case, I was in the hospital and extremely ill when a statute of limitations for filing lawsuit was about to expire. I talked to opposing counsel and informed him I was in the hospital and extremely ill and would be filing the complaint when I was well as he had stated he was not inclined to settle at the time and the statute was running, Believing because of my illness he was waiving time to file, and being extremely ill, I didn't think about the matter anymore. Imagine my surprise when I called him a day after the statute expired and his response was, "Go ahead and file, but the statute has expired." I sputtered, started to sweat a bit, and stammered I thought he had agreed to an extension of the statute of limitations, all to no avail. I called my friend, Bob, Mr. Integrity, and asked his advice. He said did you get it in writing? I hadn't. Then he said it was defensible and asked how much the case was worth. I told about three thousand dollars, and he said it wasn't enough to fight this over, and that I should go to my client and tell her I had committed malpractice and settle the matter with her, especially since my deductible was $2,500 on my liability insurance anyway. Bob said, "It happens to everyone." He reassured me (if that is possible) that everyone commits malpractice at least once in their career as an attorney, and that he even did it once.

The client actually owed me more than $3000 on some transactional work I had done for her, so I called her and told her point blank I was sorry, that I missed the filing deadline and it was malpractice. I told her I would be happy to settle the matter by not charging her the fees for the transactional work I had done for her, but that she should consult independent counsel. The client opted not to do that, had always been reasonable about what her cause of action was worth anyway, and felt she had gotten the better of the deal. I told her to think about it for a week, which she did. Everything, absolutely everything about what transpired and our agreement was put in writing. What is the caveat here? The caveat is that it is always better to just tell the truth. If you take responsibility, and if you do the right thing, you cannot go wrong.

Personally, I have never asked a client to sign a 1542 waiver for my behalf. However, it has been standard for defendants' counsel to do this when settling with a plaintiff, for as long as I can remember. If I commit malpractice, I expect myself to take responsibility for whatever I did. Opposition hates that. It means they can't scare me.

Finally, the opinion says, "The effect of a settlement agreement between a lawyer and a client releasing all claims, known and unknown, combined with a section 1542 waiver, is a matter of contract law. In some cases, depending on the facts and circumstances, the precise language of the release, whether the client is represented by independent counsel, and the intentions of the parties in entering into the settlement agreement, the settlement agreement may result in the client's release of the lawyer from all claims, known or unknown, including any claims that the client may have against the lawyer for legal malpractice."

However, enforcing of the settlement agreement may depend on whether the client has independent counsel. So you can have the client sign the agreement, but it may not be enforceable. That question would be up to the trier of fact who will apply the laws of contract and determine whether this was an arm's length transaction, among other things, all contractual issues. Honestly, I have never considered it. Perhaps I am too confident in my abilities as counsel. When I committed malpractice, I admitted it right on the settlement document and gave fair and adequate consideration for it.

Chapter Twenty-Four
State Bar Opinion # 2001-157

Now this is an opinion close to my own interest. I hate all those old files, and I feel like I need to keep them forever. I am afraid to get rid of old computers because hard drives, even if erased, can have material retrieved from them, and I keep everything, every single case from almost the beginning of time, my fear is so great.

The issues presented in this particular opinion are: "What ethical duties does an attorney have regarding the retention of former clients' files? Is the attorney ethically required to retain the files for any specific length of time following the completion of representation?"

And the answer is: "As to original papers and other property received from a former client, including estate planning and other signed, original documents delivered under Probate Code section

You Can't Do That!

710, the attorney's duties are governed by the law relating to deposits (bailments) or by the Probate Code. With respect to other "client papers and property" to which the former client is entitled under rule 3-700, absent a previous agreement, the attorney has an obligation to make reasonable efforts to obtain the former client's consent to any disposition that would prevent the former client's taking possession of the items. If, after reasonable efforts, the attorney is unable to locate the former client or obtain instructions, the attorney may destroy the items unless he or she has reason to believe (1) that preservation of the items is required by law, or (2) that destruction of the items would cause prejudice to the client, i.e., that the items are reasonably necessary to the client's legal representation. Since the 'client papers and property' to which the former client is entitled may include a variety of items, the attorney may have an obligation to examine the file contents before the file is destroyed. No specific time period for retention of a particular item can be specified. Files in criminal matters should not be destroyed without the former client's consent while the former client is alive."

Okay, my problem is I feel certain someone will come back the minute I destroy any papers, documents and/or things and tell me that I destroyed their files; and that even though I insist I made every reasonable attempt to contact the client, the client will state I did not do this and then that issue becomes an issue for the trier of fact all by itself. The bugs will probably eat the files before I have a chance to

You Can't Do That!

throw them away—but I can't just 'throw the files away' I need to shred, burn and bury them. Yes, that is exactly how paranoid I happen to be, even though I get a new client and I need files, and those files have mysteriously disappeared and the custodian of the files and/or the former attorney either can't find them or says he has destroyed them---happened to me in a worker's compensation case—what do you do? Medical records and everything are gone. Oh well. Begin again. You could report the guy, but it wouldn't get you the original files. Maybe he did tell your client. Maybe he has a letter. It is all way, way too much.

What else does the opinion say? The opinion additionally provides that the attorney's obligations with regard to closed files are taken from rule 3-700 of the Rules of Professional Conduct and Business and Professions Code section 6068, subdivision (e). Rule 3-700(D)(1) provides that a member whose employment has terminated, that the attorney no longer represents the client, shall:

"Subject to any protective order or non-disclosure agreement, promptly release to the client, at the request of the client, all the client papers and property."

Of course, if the client has engaged other counsel, then a substitution of attorney would be in play, and all documents would go to the new counsel.

This means I am probably back to where I started with a lot of dead files, no means to really know where any of these people are,

You Can't Do That!

and therefore I have no means to use to make a reasonable attempt at notice except perhaps by publication, except for those clients I know are dead---but then do the estates of the dead clients have the right to the papers, documents, and things?

(I am also a huge conspiracy theorist, but after what has happened to me, can you blame me?)

Chapter Twenty-Five
State Bar Opinion # 2003-161

This opinion addresses the following issue: "Under what circumstances may a communication in a non-office setting by a person seeking legal services or advice from an attorney be entitled to protection as confidential client information when the attorney accepts no engagement, expresses no agreement as to confidentiality, and assumes no responsibility over any matter?"

The answer is that person's communication made to an attorney in a non-office setting can result in an attorney obligation to preserve confidentiality whether or not an attorney-client relationship is created. The attorney's words or actions may cause the non-attorney to have a reasonable belief he or she is consulting the attorney in confidence or in a professional capacity to retain the attorney or to obtain legal services or advice.

You Can't Do That!

This is why you need to keep your mouth shut about the law in any social situation, because loose lips really do sink ships, and not only may you be perceived as receiving a confidential communication, you may be liable for giving off the cuff legal advice that turns out to be wrong and ultimately find yourself in a court of law being sued for malpractice!

The state bar used the following authorities in formulating its opinion: Rule 3-310(E) of the Rules of Professional Conduct of the State Bar of California. Business and Professions Code section 6068, subdivision (e), and Evidence Code sections 951, 952, and 954.

"An attorney-client relationship, together with all the attendant duties a lawyer owes a client, including the duty of confidentiality, may be created by contract, either express or implied."

An implied contract can be found if there exists a belief by the non-attorney that a relationship was formed and that the relationship could be reasonably induced by the representations or conduct of the attorney. The factors that will be considered in evaluating whether an attorney-client relationship exists will be whether the attorney volunteered his advice, whether the attorney agreed to investigate a matter and provide legal advice on possible merits of a case, did the attorney previously represent the individual, was legal advice sought and given, was the setting confidential, and were fees or other consideration given the attorney for advice.

You Can't Do That!

California Evidence Code section 952 defines confidential communications between a client and lawyer as information exchanged between a client and his or her lawyer in the course of that relationship in confidence by a means which, so far as the client is aware, discloses the information to no third party other than those present to further the interest of the client in the consultation or to whom disclosure is reasonably necessary. The code specifies communications between client and lawyer are not deemed "lacking in confidentiality" because communication is by facsimile, cellular telephone, or other electronic means. The confidentiality is found in the reasonable interpretation of totality of the circumstances.

Therefore, the bottom line is even if you think a person is not a client, if you give them advice, they may think they are your client and the confidentiality rule will apply.

CHAPTER TWENTY-SIX
State Bar Opinion # 1993-133

The question answered in this opinion is, "May a lawyer who has successfully defended B in a lawsuit brought by A, thereafter represent A in a malpractice action against A's attorney which resulted in the loss of the lawsuit against B?"

The answer is "B's attorney may not communicate with A about the subject of the representation without the consent of A's counsel, unless A is no longer represented by counsel in the matter. Before B's attorney may represent A in the malpractice claim against A's former attorney, B's attorney must provide A with a written disclosure of the relevant circumstances and the actual and potential adverse consequences to A by reason of the representation of B. The disclosure should include the prospect of both B and B's attorney being witnesses in the malpractice action. B's attorney must also obtain the informed written consent of B, and if B continues to be a client, the attorney must obtain the written consent of both A and B. It is unlikely the attorney can comply with his or her obligation to provide A with written disclosure under rule 3-310(B) without B's consent to disclosure of any confidential information relevant to the representation of A. This Committee believes it would be imprudent for B's lawyer to accept the representation of A in a legal malpractice action against A's former attorney where the negligence of A's attorney resulted in the loss of the case against B. A's malpractice claim under these facts presupposes that A's claim against B was meritorious and that if A's attorney had handled the case properly, A would have prevailed against B. A lawyer who undertakes to represent a party in a matter which is inconsistent with lawyer's duties to a client or former client and which creates the potential for a disclosure of the former client's confidences opens the lawyer to claims of unprofessional conduct."

The authorities used in making the decision were Rules 2-100, 3-310 and 5-210 of the Rules of Professional Conduct along with Business and Professions Code section 6068, subdivision (e).

I quoted this abbreviation of the opinion because it reminds me of the old who's on first bit. It is like a merry-go-round, and the logic seems all too obvious. It makes me laugh. Now I am thinking over in my own mind how opposing counsel tried to set a wedge between me and my client in the fraudulent conveyance/title

You Can't Do That!

insurance case I discussed earlier. By stating in their papers I was willfully soliciting to set aside the deed of my client by bringing an action to quiet title and by further saying to the court and to my client that I had committed malpractice (for which they had no standing to even say, they were actually admitting a fraud existed, because absent the fraud, there would be no need to quiet title; and I couldn't possibly be willfully soliciting to set aside the deed of my client, because it would mean nothing at all, just a quiet title. Of course, the facts were set forth in the complaint in their entirety, with the various causes of action. The underlying issues were to be decided by the trier of fact. But in saying if no one was told they never would have found out, they were indeed making an admission of wrong as well as presenting a position contrary to the interests of their own clients. I can only wonder why the court got so confused. I do believe I argued that. As they say hindsight is fantastic.

That must be the reason they wanted to get rid of me so vehemently, or at least it must have been one of the reasons. On paper they were in violation of the Rules of Professional Conduct, not to mention what they were doing to me as opposition counsel.

I love this opinion! I think I'll remember it!

You Can't Do That!

CHAPTER TWENTY-SEVEN
State Bar Opinion # 1989-116

The question posed in this opinion is, "May an attorney-client retainer agreement include a provision for mandatory binding arbitration of potential malpractice claims against the attorney?"

And the answer to that question is "There is no prohibition against an attorney-client retainer agreement requiring arbitration of potential malpractice claims. Where there is no preexisting attorney-client relationship between the parties, the extent to which the client is fully advised of the terms and consequences of the arbitration provision and knowingly consents to it goes to the legal enforceability rather than the ethical propriety of the provision. However, where there is a preexisting attorney-client relationship, the attorney has an ethical duty apart from any legal duty to assure that the client is fully aware of and knowingly consents to the terms and consequences of the arbitration provision the attorney seeks to negotiate with the client."

Therefore, again it appears the best thing you can do is to be very specific and complete in your transactional contractual agreements with your clients. The state bar uses as its authority in formulating this opinion, rules 3-300, 3-310 and 3-400 of the Rules of Professional Conduct of the State Bar of California, California Evidence Code section 951 and California Code of Civil Procedure sections 1141.10, 1280 et seq. and 1295. (Please look for updated versions of these these codes, statutes and rules as they may have changed---however, I want to give you the authority exactly as it was cited in the event you want to see the original text upon which the State Bar of California relied in reaching its decision.)

The reasoning of the state bar is that public policy supports and favors arbitration agreements. California Code of Civil Procedure section 1141.10 declares the legislative intent of California's judicial arbitration procedure by stating:

"The Legislature. . . finds and declares that arbitration has proven to be an efficient and equitable method for resolving small claims, and that courts should encourage or require the use of arbitration for such actions whenever possible."

Arbitration of a wide variety of claims including professional negligence claims is statutorily favored. Doctors use this clause in their treatment agreements on a regular basis and my even refuse to treat you if you refuse to sign and agree to arbitration in the event of a claim you may want to make later for malpractice. In fact, they will tell you their malpractice (liability) insurance requires they place this clause in their agreements, if you bother to ask them.

As for attorneys, it is probably a good idea to put the arbitration clause in your agreements to represent them in a legal matter, no matter how small or insignificant the matter may be, because arbitration will be far less costly (if you end up being ordered to pay) and less time consuming, meaning you will have more time to devote in the long term to other matters, whatever those matters may be.

Now, I don't like the so called auto insurance "in house" arbitrations where you are never allowed to face your accuser, and some seemingly invisible independent arbitrator behind closed doors reviews facts given him by two insurers. I don't trust that, and never will trust that being the conspiracy theorist I am. At some point I think this will be blown apart, because you have no opportunity to be heard; and if you are found at fault, your insurance rates may go up in a taking of the worst kind. Also, they put these points against you that are separate from the DMV points, and they sit as both judge and jury over you with (in my opinion) little or no understanding of the law and how it should be applied.

Perhaps attorneys and judges don't know everything about the law anyway, but at least they went to law school and passed a bar examination and can therefore do more than an adjuster with little or no training when it comes to the particular nuances of the law, rather than saying any time you turn left (for example) you are at fault—when the law gives exceptions as to when the right of way shifts---

In any event, arbitration is great and the court may order you into non-binding arbitration, or you may elect to have binding arbitration in many cases, so why not just skip the court part and put it directly into your fee agreement because it makes sense. Your professional liability carrier may even require it.

Chapter Twenty-Eight
State Bar Opinion # 1991-194

The question answered by this opinion is "Is it ethically proper for counsel retained by a client in a civil matter to send a letter to the opposing side stating that unless a prompt and satisfactory settlement is reached "all available legal remedies will be pursued?"

The answer to the question is yes.

Rule of Professional Conduct 5-100 states in pertinent part:) "A member shall not threaten to present criminal, administrative, or disciplinary charges to obtain an advantage in a civil dispute."

The meaning of the proposed language that "all available legal remedies will be pursued" unless a satisfactory settlement is promptly forthcoming, is ambiguous. Because it is ambiguous it can't constitute a threat, and so this is all you should ever say and it is as clear as you can get into matters with the opposition unless you want to be accused of making a treat.

Basically, even if a civil dispute isn't pending and even if your intent is to inform someone they have committed a criminal act and to help them correct the problem and to stop the furtherance of criminal activities, you cannot do this or say anything if there is a possibility that a civil action will ensue. Do not send the opposition penal code sections. Do not pass go. Do not collect two hundred dollars. Just say, "all legal remedies will be pursued." Then hold your breath and find out if opposing counsel will do the same thing. Even if you think the person is your friend, do not tell them anything other than that.

Now if it is your child? I would say something and correct the problem. Besides, you aren't likely to bring a lawsuit against your own child. But if you discover anything else about any other person, whether or not they are completely ignorant they are committing a criminal act, keep your mouth shut.

If you think I am talking about the embezzler in the case of the two child molesters and the embezzler, you are right. I will not discuss this any further. I do think in some ways not being able to fully communicate with the opposition does a disservice to getting what needs to be accomplished done, and for me, ever since this rule came out, I seem to be accused of everything and at the same time I have to watch everything I say. The reason is many civil acts are

You Can't Do That!

also criminal acts, such as a fraudulent conveyance, for example, which also comes under the penal code. Everyone thinks this is just a civil matter, but fraud can be both criminal and civil---all kinds of frauds---You are allowed to tell someone in a family law matter that you may be filing contempt against them, and that is also a criminal matter because it could cause a person to be incarcerated, but that is okay, and nothing else is. It also used to be that you could lay out all the applicable law for your opposition and that wasn't considered a threat, but now it is. I suppose it all really boils down to the interpretation of what is overt, what does an overt threat mean? Basically, if you tell them it is there, you are threatening them. So all you can do is say either all available legal remedies will be pursued or scream as loudly as you can "You Can't do that!" (Both statements seem equally ambiguous---just don't tell anyone why they can't do it, just to be safe, unless of course you are an officer of the law.) Now if the other guys would just stop threatening me with everything under the sun, I would be a happy camper.

You Can't Do That!

CHAPTER TWENTY-NINE
State Bar Opinion # 1987-92

In order to spice up this book just a little bit (if that is possible) and to get you thinking about the meaning of prurient interests I chose this opinion which poses the eternal and you should already know the answer to this question, "What are the ethical considerations of a lawyer engaging in a sexual relationship with a client?"

And the answer is (drum roll please) "No California Rule of Professional Conduct expressly prohibits a lawyer from having a sexual relationship with a client. However, such conduct could in some circumstances give rise to a violation of rules 6-101 or 5-102. In addition, such conduct might present a question as to a client's ability to consent to a sexual relationship and also could detrimentally impact on the client's ability to render independent judgments in the professional relationship. Finally, such conduct must be evaluated in light of Business and Professions Code section 6068."

To which I say, "Surprise!"

Current Rule 3-120 states an attorney cannot "require or demand sexual relations with a client incident to or as a condition of *any* professional representation; or employ coercion, intimidation, or undue influence in entering into sexual relations with a client; or continue representation of a client with whom the member has sexual relations if such sexual relations cause the member to perform legal services incompetently in violation of rule 3-110." (Numbering omitted,)

Now I would have thought out of my own common sense the bar would prohibit sexual relations with a client, and I would really worry about anyone that did have sexual relations with a client as to where this might lead. In fact, the rules state in discussion of this rule that Rule 3-120 is intended to prohibit sexual exploitation by a lawyer in the course of a professional representation. So if the intent is to prohibit, why does this opinion say there is no specific rule prohibiting sexual relationships between attorney and client, and why isn't the intent stated more specifically? While the conversation over this may lie in the technicalities, it would seem that this type of thing is prohibited under only certain circumstances. However, are you willing to let a twarted lover blur the line you thought was there.

You Can't Do That!

What is that saying? It is, "There is nothing like a woman scorned." So be very careful boys and girls, especially you boys!

The proposed new rules that have not as of the date of this writing, been accepted by the California Supreme Court, state under Rule 1.8.10, Sexual Relations With Client, part (a) "A lawyer shall not engage in sexual relations with a client unless a consensual sexual relationship existed between them when the lawyer-client relationship commenced."

And when and if the PROPOSED RULES OF PROFESSIONAL CONDUCT, adopted by the Board of Governors on July 24, 2010 and September 22, 2010 are approved by the Supreme Court of the State of California, that *should* clear up matters considerably.

Between now and then, it is my strong suggestion that you comply with the proposed rules in order to avoid the appearance of any impropriety with regard to this salacious matter that could get you in deep trouble with the State Bar of California.

Chapter Thirty
It's Just The Rules, Ma'am

There really aren't that many rules to follow, and of those rules, not all of them will apply to you. I will admit that sometimes it's hard to keep track of things, and sometimes the rules may not be as specific as we like. But I have decided the reason I have had all of these things happen to me was so I could get to know the rules better. They are second nature to me now. . . like breathing out and breathing in (to reminisce from the musical 'My Fair Lady'). And while Henry Higgin's question was, "Why can't the English learn to speak?" my question is, "Why can't the legal community follow the rules?"

The short answer is, "We can!" We can follow The Rules of Professional Conduct. We can have integrity, and we can be responsible and we can be all that we were meant to be when we first took our oaths before the state bar and the court. Yes, it is annoying the rules keep changing and the law keeps changing and the world keeps changing, but that is just a part of life. It is sort of like the seasons we don't have in Southern California.

Perhaps we should follow the advice of my mother and simply follow the Golden Rule. Now that is a rule that covers every other rule: "Do unto others as you would have others do onto you."

When I was an elementary school teacher I had only three rules for my kids:

1. Don't do anything to hurt yourself.
2. Don't do anything to hurt another person.
3. Don't destroy the property of another.

Now those three rules would pretty much serve anyone well, and that is why I gave these same rules to my own children. They were given to me by an old master teacher of mine, a teacher who taught teachers to teach, and nothing made more sense than that. The rules are simple and easy to remember and very easy to apply to any situation. They work. You don't have to think too much about which rules to remember, and I think these rules would pretty much cover any situation.

You Can't Do That!

The problem is attorneys generally want to hurt the other side, they end up hurting themselves, and the property of another is inevitably lost, taken or destroyed.

If we all just thought about the other side in a manner consistent with truth and integrity, we wouldn't have these problems. Practicing law should not just be about winning. It should be about compromise and doing the right thing. We should seek fair amounts in damages, not ridiculous amounts so we can get a higher contingency fee. In criminal matters we should be honest with our clients. I had a client once that liked to tell everyone how I sent him to jail, and it changed his life. He said he would have been dead if I hadn't sent him to jail. Well, I didn't exactly send him to jail. What I did was I encouraged him to accept responsibility for his wrong, got him to accept he had done wrong, and worked with the court to get him a fair sentence in combination with drug rehabilitation. This was a nineteen year old kid, and he learned something about doing the right thing. Sure, I may have been able to get the guy off, but then he would just feel as though he had gotten away with something and he would do it again. This was not the first time I had done this with a client. The result has been absolutely no repeat offenders. And the odd thing is these people recommended me to other people, because they knew I really cared about them as people, not just fees in my pocket.

You Can't Do That!

This is how I like to practice law. Perhaps it is the mothering approach to law, but praying with my client and for my client---to let God guide us through the process--even with unbelievers, is both important and memorable. Of course, I give them all the options, but in the cases I have had in this arena (mostly drug cases) taking responsibility seems to be the first step in getting well.

If there happens to be a possible civil case entwined with your talk about responsibility; however, this could get you into some trouble. For me, if a case is complex in that way, I send it on to someone more experienced in those matters with the caveat that I will help where I can if needed.

I am a great rule follower. I think rules and the law are very good things indeed. I am obsessive, compulsive about right and justice, about doing the right thing. I still believe that you come into the law with all your morals and values in place, whatever they may be. I think there are many amoral people out there who feed off other amoral people. These people will ridicule you for your values and your beliefs. They will attack in hordes if they get the chance. They will do anything to win. They have threatened to do anything to get rid of me. Why do they do this? They do this because I am a threat to their way of life and law practice. I take it as a compliment. If the hairs are raised on the back of the opposition's neck it is because they feel they are cornered, and it is a fight between right and wrong. It would be nice if right always came out the winner, but that is not always the case.

I have tried a little bit of almost every area of the law, and the only place where the attorneys are generally civil is in the probate court. I figure that's because just about everyone concerned is dead. The guys in probate have tans. They are relaxed. When I did a trial in probate my opponent said, "I don't know who is telling the truth, your client or mine. Let's just let the judge decide." I didn't know who was telling the truth either. It was nice to have an honest opponent who was more worried about the truth than winning the case. I didn't have to stop and scream "You Can't do that!" We were just in search of the truth, and the search for truth should be what the law is.

The above and this entire book is the opinion of one attorney and it is not meant to give specific advise on any area of the law. For specific advice on any area of the law you should consult your own attorney. When I did, I was glad. You will be glad as well.

The law is all about the truth, the whole truth, and nothing but the truth, so help me God.

You Can't Do That!

"To see what is right and not to do it is want of courage."

Confucius

Appendix

Material for this book came, in part, from the following cites with permission by license:

1. Excerpt of The State Bar of California Standing Committee on Professional Responsibility and Conduct (COPRAC) Formal Opinion Number 2009-178 © 2010 The State Bar of California. All Rights Reserved. For the full text of the opinion, see <u>www.calbar.ca.gov</u>. (Go to "Ethics")

2. Excerpt of The State Bar of California Standing Committee on Professional Responsibility and Conduct (COPRAC) Formal Opinion Number 2001-157 © 2010 The State Bar of California. All Rights Reserved. For the full text of the opinion, see <u>www.calbar.ca.gov</u>. (Go to "Ethics")

3. Excerpt of The State Bar of California Standing Committee on Professional Responsibility and Conduct (COPRAC) Formal Opinion Number 2001-157 © 2010 The State Bar of California. All Rights Reserved. For the full text of the opinion, see <u>www.calbar.ca.gov</u>. (Go to "Ethics")

4. Excerpt of The State Bar of California Standing Committee on Professional Responsibility and Conduct (COPRAC) Formal Opinion Number 2003-161 © 2010 The State Bar of California. All Rights Reserved. For the full text of the opinion, see <u>www.calbar.ca.gov</u>. (Go to "Ethics")

5. Excerpt of The State Bar of California Standing Committee on Professional Responsibility and Conduct (COPRAC) Formal Opinion Number 1993-133 © 2010 The State Bar of California. All Rights Reserved. For the full text of the opinion, see <u>www.calbar.ca.gov</u>. (Go to "Ethics")

6. Excerpt of The State Bar of California Standing Committee on Professional Responsibility and Conduct (COPRAC) Formal Opinion Number 1989-116 © 2010 The State Bar of California. All Rights

Reserved. For the full text of the opinion, see www.calbar.ca.gov. (Go to "Ethics")

7. *Excerpt of The State Bar of California Standing Committee on Professional Responsibility and Conduct (COPRAC) Formal Opinion Number1987-92 © 2010 The State Bar of California. All Rights Reserved. For the full text of the opinion, see www.calbar.ca.gov. (Go to "Ethics"*

8. *Excerpt of The State Bar of California Standing Committee on Professional Responsibility and Conduct (COPRAC) Formal Opinion Number 1991-194 © 2010 The State Bar of California. All Rights Reserved. For the full text of the opinion, see www.calbar.ca.gov. (Go to "Ethics")*

9. *Excerpts from The State Bar of California Attorney Guidelines of Civility and Professionalism Adopted by the Board of Governors on July 20, 2007 © 2010 The State Bar of California. All Rights Reserved.* **SECTION 1.RESPONSIBILITIES TO THE JUSTICE SYSTEM.** *See full test at www.calbar.ca.gov. (Go to "Ethics")*

10. *Excerpts from The State Bar of California Attorney Guidelines of Civility and Professionalism Adopted by the Board of Governors on July 20, 2007* **SECTION 6: SCHEDULING, CONTINUANCES AND EXTENSIONS OF TIME.** *© 2010 The State Bar of California. All Rights Reserved. See full test at www.calbar.ca.gov. (Go to "Ethics")*

11. *Excerpts from The State Bar of California* **PROPOSED RULES OF PROFESSIONAL CONDUCT** *(Adopted by the Board of Governors on July 24, 2010 and September 22, 2010. © 2010 The State Bar of California. All Rights Reserved. Rules of Professional Conduct must be approved by the Supreme Court of California in order to become operative. Rule 1.8.1 Business Transactions with a Client and Acquiring Interests Adverse to the Clien---See full test at www.calbar.ca.gov. (Go to "Ethics")*

12. *Excerpts from The State Bar of California* **CALIFORNIA RULES**

You Can't Do That!

OF PROFESSIONAL CONDUCT 2010 CURRENT RULES *(Current rules as of January 1, 2010. Rule 1-320, Rule 1-310, Rule 1-311, Rule 1-500, Rule 1-700, Rule 3-100, 3-310, Rule 3-210, Rule 3-410, 3-400, Rule 3-510, Rule 3-500, Rule 5-200, Rule 5-100, Rule 5-101, Rule 1-311, Rule 1-310, Rule 1-320.* © *2010 The State Bar of California. All Rights Reserved. See full test at www.calbar.ca.gov. (Go to "Ethics")*

13. Excerpts from The State Bar of California RULES OF PROFESSIONAL CONDUCT 2010 CURRENT RULES *(Current rules as of January 1, 2010. The following statement from the beginning of the rules:*

"The following rules are intended to regulate professional conduct of members of the State Bar through discipline. They have been adopted by the Board of Governors of the State Bar of California and approved by the Supreme Court of California pursuant to Business and professions Code sections 6076 and 6077 to protect the public and to promote respect and confidence in the legal profession. These rules together with any standards adopted by the Board of Governors pursuant to these rules shall be binding upon all members of the State Bar."

© *2010 The State Bar of California. All Rights Reserved. See full test at www.calbar.ca.gov. (Go to "Ethics")*

www.ingramcontent.com/pod-product-compliance
Ingram Content Group UK Ltd.
Pitfield, Milton Keynes, MK11 3LW, UK
UKHW022232230426
12048UKWH00016BA/1201